C000097116

Slice of Kent

56 recipes celebrating the food of Kent by its finest chefs

Sign up to our newsletter to receive information on our next book featuring more casual restaurants in Kent, new restaurant openings, special dinners, products and offers.
different-perspective.co.uk/kent

Follow us on Instagram
david_pearce_publisher

different-perspective.co.uk

First Edition
Oliver Cameron Publishing Ltd
Staplehurst
Kent TN12 0JT

www.different-perspective.co.uk

Written by David Pearce
Photography by David Pearce
Design by Colin Butcher
Cover Art by Carole Aston

ISBN - 9780956546388

FOREWORD

Kent is my home and buried deep in my heart. I never thought I would end up coming back to work in Kent after 20 years in London, but now I've settled in Folkestone I couldn't think of anywhere else I would want to bring up my kids.

I met David whilst we were at college and then worked at the celebrated Reads Restaurant together for many years. He was an expert in wine, both in knowledge and how to drink it of course!! Like me David has a passion for Kent and this prompted him to produce this stunning book.

Kent has some of the best produce in the country and is sometimes overlooked, but apart from being famous for our soft fruits and apples, we have fantastic salt marsh lamb, orchard reared pigs, beautiful chickens and a wealth of game, not to mention plenty of grass to rear beautiful beef. Lets not forget also that the whole of Kent is surrounded by water meaning stunning fish and seafood is available in abundance and amazing quality.

In this book David showcases a number of the finest restaurants in the county and there are many. With produce as good as this stunning county supplies its brilliant to see so many talented chefs making the most of it.

Thanks David for bringing my beloved county to life.

Mark Sargeant

INTRODUCTION

Kent has been home for my entire life, but like so many, I have been fortunate enough to travel quite extensively through pleasure and work, introducing me to a plethora of regional cuisines. Given the choice, the option of a trip that incorporates an element of food over sitting on a beach all day; you can guess which I would choose. With such low airfares now it is possible to escape the UK for lunch in Copenhagen, Jerez or a host of other cities, as I have. This book, however, is about celebrating the food of Kent, and my love for it.

Allow me to indulge myself by giving a little background to my formative years and how I became involved with food and why I have written this book. I was not born into a family that went out to restaurants. I have no recollection of eating in a proper restaurant until I was maybe 15, and only then because I was working in one...

My mum (widowed at 39) sent me to Dulwich College in Cranbrook as a full time boarder for five years, but I would always look forward to coming home and enjoying her food. Everything was fresh, healthy and nutritious, not that I had an understanding of such things. I particularly enjoyed mum's slow-cooked liver stew, as well as my grans Sunday roasts, followed by sherry trifle, which I would happily polish off three portions of!

I was not academic, and probably regressed after starting at my local comprehensive in Maidstone, having left DCPS. It was decided that a career in hospitality would be ideal for me (my school suggested a YTS scheme) so I chose to undertake work experience in Larkfield Priory, a Trust House Forte hotel. I found this to be very enjoyable, not only as I was interacting with people through general duties, but through the responsibility I was given at the age of 14. That the guests of TV's *No 73* show stayed there also helped. Meeting all the big pop stars of the day was certainly a privilege.

Skipping forward a couple of years, the manager heard I was at West Kent College studying catering, and suggested I work in the restaurant as a waiter. Reluctantly I agreed, but soon discovered that I loved it. A defining moment for me came after a year when a guest requested a Beaujolais and the waitress explained we did not stock any. I was sure we did and after checking the wine list my inkling was right - we had Fleurie. This was the moment of realisation that I had more than a passing interest in wine.

At college I soon became great friends with a classmate by the name of Mark Sargeant. For two years I chauffeured him to college (I was a year older and had a car) during which time we had to go on work placement one day a week. We were sent to a famous castle in Kent and set to work in the café. We lasted one day before we told our lecturer, Mr Avery, that it didn't suit us. We wanted to work in fine dining and this was not it. He suggested we call David and Rona Pitchford at Reads Restaurant in Faversham to ask if they might take us on. We were invited to visit and we must have impressed them. Mark talking about food and the likes of Macro Pierre White, and me obsessing over the wine list and in particular Bordeaux. I don't think they had ever dreamed two likely 17 year old lads from Maidstone would have this passion for food-and-wine. It was 1989 and the food scene was pretty much non existent in Kent.

We both loved our work placement and ended up working at Reads (I think Mark went to London first though for a bit - again with me playing chauffeur.) We talked food 18 hours a day - it was as if there was nothing else except food to discuss! We decided that one day we would open a restaurant together called "Circles" (which I am still waiting to do Mark!).

Rona and David were exceptional in helping us develop our careers by involving us in experiences outside of the restaurant. We accompanied them in 1992 to the Roux Brothers 25-year celebration at Langans Brasserie, where Michael Aspel came out with the famous *This Is Your Life* red book. The private event was by invitation only and attended by the great and the good of the industry. It was such a privilege to be there. On other occasions we would visit France or go on holiday together, eating some wonderful food.

One of the best aspects of working at Reads was the Grub Tin. Literally every member of staff would put in £2 per week and twice a year we would go out to lunch somewhere special. This was the early 1990's remember, so this usually meant a trip to London, as Kent was still a culinary desert. We ate at Le Gavroche, Harveys, Nico at 90, La Tante Claire, The Capital Hotel, Le Manoir, L'Ortolan and The Waterside Inn. It was always humorous paying the not-insignificant bill in £1 coins! These lunches gave an incredible insight to the heights fine dining and accompanying service could reach. I would often eat at those restaurants on my day off. My friends spent their money drinking lager on a Saturday night in clubs, while I chose to dine in two and three starred Michelin restaurants on a Monday.

The day the new Michelin guide came out was always nerve wracking, especially as we were striving for a star. One year Rona informed me that Michelin had retracted our Red M (this was a notch below a star). I was emotionally devastated - it was something we had all worked so hard to achieve. Thankfully, Rona went onto explain that we could not have a Red M as we had been awarded a star! Writing this now, more than 25 years later, I can still feel those emotions well up inside. It was incredible. It was just myself Rona and I think Becky, at the time working front of house, and so we gave each guest a glass of Champagne that lunchtime.

In those days there were only 43 restaurants in the whole of England that had been awarded a star, so it was an incredible achievement.

We were fortunate to have some wonderful guests, some of whom are friends to this day (Alistair and Maggie). They would talk about food and new places to try in the ever expanding culinary landscape. I particularly enjoyed serving guests who would ask for a wine recommendation. It was my purpose as a career sommelier to advise and help guests make the right choice for them.

The art of a good sommelier is not to try and up-sell. It is to find out what you enjoy drinking and make suggestions based on that and within your budget. I would always encourage guests to try something they might not be familiar with, but something I thought they would enjoy. To me, food and wine matching should not be complex but simple. Primarily, enjoy what you like but be open to suggestions.

This openess is one factor that attratced me to my wife, Sarah. I had taken her to Reims, in the Champagne area of France shortly after we met, as a guest of a Grande Marque Champagne house. Having sabred the top of a bottle off with great theatre we proceeded to lunch. This had been pre-arranged with accompanying wines. The main course was steak tartare (raw steak and egg) which I love but had no idea how Sarah, a 22 year old, not from a culinary background, would respond. She loved it - much to my delight.

I am pleased our son James (now grown up and graduated) is also adventurous in his eating. I recall trips to France with him requesting items unfamililar to the British palate which made me immensely proud.

The dining scene in the UK is now so vibrant that it is almost impossible to keep up. We have enough restaurants with Michelin stars to eat at a different one three times a week for a year. It is not all about stars and nor should it be.

What is so exciting is the sheer number of fantastic chefs in their 20's and 30's working in Kent currently. They are passionate, hungry for success and pushing themselves. With the internet and explosion of Instagram, they are incredibly fortunate to see what their peers are cooking almost on a daily basis. This pushes them to strive for excellence in their kitchens, but they need a solid foundation and skill set to draw from. All too often I see ambition that exceeds ability.

The number of producers of food and drink in Kent has to be at an all-time high. There truly is an amazing array of produce on offer in the many farm shops, delis and markets. By reading this book, you are probably already a consumer at many of them. I therefore ask you to encourage your friends to join you in swapping larger commercial brands to smaller artisan products, that invariably have more soul, flavour and provenance that is so often missing. These are often cottage businesses founded out of passion. They deserve to be sampled and supported. We have a number of food fairs in Kent which provide an ideal opportunity to discover them.

The only item grow outside of Kent that I truly love is truffles. My great friends Andy and Amy live in rural Umbria, Italy and are surrounded by them in season. Hunted by Franco and Paolo with their truffle dogs, it is always magical to visit and experience their incredible hospitality and genorosity (and also Monia's Negronis, which I love!). If anyone can figure out how to get truffles to spore and grow in Kent then I will be your biggest customer...

A number of wineries such as Terlingham Vineyard or Woodchurch Wines are open to the public. It is a great opportunity to chat with the winemakers at the same time as sampling and buying a selection of their wines. Why not make a day of it and enjoy lunch at one of the restaurants featured here or visit Whitstable to try their world-famous oysters?

This book has very much been a passion project (no restaurants or producers have paid to be in here) so I am very grateful to you for reading it.

I hope you get pleasure and knowledge from this book. I firmly believe that not everything should be handed to you on a plate. As home cooks we need to be brave on occasion and make choices. It is with this is mind, I have not altered the chefs recipes. They have provided as much information that they believe you need. If you find that it is not enough then please use your intuition. I promise you will become a better cook because of it.

David Pearce

Sides - greens s[...]

Junket + honeycomb [...]
Apple crumble, creme an[...]
Flourless chocolate cake, salted [...]
Sticky date pudding, creme [...]
Atkinson, Wagners + [...]

Angela's of

Angela's of
Margate

Margate

"_Minimising our impact on our environment is essential to the work we do. That can range from cutting waste by working with growers, fishermen and suppliers who understand how to make the most of their produce to almost eliminating all plastic from our restaurant._"

Rob Cooper - Angela's of Margate

HAKE, PARSNIP AND SHELLFISH SAUCE

Pan-roasted hake on the bone served with a parsnip mash and a shellfish sauce

Hake is a sustainanble alternative to Cod. It doesn't have quite the same smoothness but holds strong sauces equally well and works so well in this recipe

Ingredients

Fish stock

1kg fish bones like turbot, sole, brill, hake.
Washed and all blood gone.
Water to cover.

Shellfish stock (makes 500ml)

1kg of either chopped shell-on prawns, langoustine, crab or lobster carcasses
2 white onions chopped
2 carrots chopped
2 heads celery chopped
6 ripe tomatoes chopped
6 garlic cloves chopped
1 star anis
1 tablespoon smoked paprika
50ml rapeseed oil

Shellfish sauce (makes 300ml)

500ml fish stock
500ml shellfish stock
6 ripe tomatoes chopped
1 star anis
Pinch saffron strands
50g unsalted butter
Maldon sea salt
Cayenne pepper
Lemon juice

To make the sauce involves three preparations. They can all be done in advance.

Parsnips
Potatoes
Milk
4 x 140g hake steaks

Serves 4

> *In this recipe treat the hake as you would a T-bone steak. It is first roasted in the pan, while being constantly basted in plenty of butter and its own juices. This creates a deep rich flavour in the fish*

Method

Fish stock. Pre-heat oven to 200°C. Roast the fish bones on a flat oven tray for 30 mins. Turn over and roast for a further 10 mins. Empty into a stock pot with enough water to cover. Bring to a simmer for 30mins and skim off any impurities with a spoon as you go. Remove from the heat and strain through a sieve into another pan and reduce rapidly by half. Take off the heat and allow to cool. Stock is now ready to use and can be stored for up to three days in the fridge or three months in the freezer.

Shellfish stock. Pre heat oven to 200°C. Roast the shellfish on a flat oven tray for 30 mins (40mins if using crab or lobster). Meanwhile, sweat down all the other ingredients in 50ml of rapeseed oil in a stock pot for about 5 mins or until lightly coloured. Once the shellfish is roasted, add to the sweated veg and add water to cover. Simmer for an hour skimming any impurities off with a spoon. After an hour strain through a sieve into another pan - pushing hard with a ladle to extract as much liquid as possible. Reduce rapidly by half. Take off the heat and allow to cool. The stock is now ready to use and can be stored for up to 3 days in the fridge or 3 months in the freezer.

Pour both stocks into a large pan and add the tomatoes, star anis, saffron and butter. Bring to a simmer and reduce to 200ml. Tip into a liquidiser or use a stick blender to blitz the sauce for 2 mins. Pass through a fine sieve pushing through with a ladle to extract all the sauce. Return to the heat and season with the salt, lemon, and if you like heat, some cayenne to taste. The sauce is now ready to use and can be stored for up to three days in the fridge or three months in the freezer.

Parsnip mash. Boil the parsnips and potatoes in milk with a pinch of salt. When cooked drain through a colander over another pan, reserving the milk. Mash the parsnips and potatoes with the butter and add a splash of the cooking milk if they seem a bit dry. Season to taste.

Hake steaks: Ask your fishmonger for four steaks cut from the centre of the fish weighing about 140g. Pre-heat a skillet pan and pan roast for 2 mins, constantly basting in butter until the skin is crispy. Transfer them to the oven and roast for 6-8 mins or until cooked – the flesh should just pull away from the bone. Season with a pinch of sea salt and baste with any cooking juices. Rest for 6 mins.

Sweat down a handful of Swiss chard or spinach in a knob of butter until nice and tender.

RAY KNOBS, PUMPKIN AND COBNUT

Pan-fried 'poor man's scallops' with crown prince pumpkin and roasted cobnuts

One of the fisherman's treats that is not usually requested but ray knobs are such incredibly juicy morsels of meat that they really should be used more

Ingredients

20 Thornback ray knobs
700g crown prince pumpkin peeled
de-seeded & chopped into 1cm dice
100g cobnuts shelled
50g butter diced

Ray Knobs are incredibly tender, delicate pieces of fish. Don't eat the small piece of cartilage though!

Method

Pre-heat oven to 180°C.

On a flat oven tray roast 300g chopped pumpkin for 10 mins. Set aside.

On a flat oven tray roast the cobnuts until golden (about 10 mins). Set aside.

Put the remaining 400g chopped pumpkin in a saucepan and cover with water. Add a pinch of salt and simmer gently for 15 mins or until soft. Strain over another pan through a sieve to reserve the juice and mash the cooked pumpkin with the butter until smooth. If it feels too dry, incorporate a little of the reserved cooking liquor.

Pre-heat a large skillet pan to a medium hot temperature and pan fry the knobs for 4 mins on one side before carefully turning them over and finishing for a further 2 mins. Turn off the heat and leave the knobs to rest in the residue heat of the pan with 50g of butter and a squeeze of lemon for a further 2 mins. Warm the cobnuts and the roasted pumpkin back through the oven and reheat the purée.

Spoon some purée onto the centre of the plate. Share the knobs out - five per plate - onto the purée and scatter the garnish of nuts and roast pumpkin over the top. Finish with a drizzle of pan juice.

Angela's of
Margate

**Maria Cocconi
Buenos Aires Nights**

"*Argentine cuisine may be described as the cultural blend and influenced by Italian and Spanish populations. Argentine people have a reputation for their love of best steak. Cooking a steak to perfection takes time. We are not a fast-food restaurant and all our food is made fresh, with our cooking techniques being slow heat. It is not high tempratures and fast cooking to avoid any burning taste and to concetrate the flavour.*"

Maria Cocconi - Buenos Aires Nights

SEA BASS
Sweet potato wedges

Food is not simply something that people eat when they are hungry. Food is inspiring, and so much more, bring people together and creating good memories

Ingredients

1 fillet of sea bass
2 sweet potatoes wedges
1 basil leaves, finely chopped
30ml vermouth rosso
60ml Chardonnay wine
3 button mushroom, sliced
80g leek, sliced
½ tbsp butter
Olive oil
Salt and pepper

Perfect dish to pair with a good glass of Pinot Grigio or a glass of Viognier

Method

Pre-heat the oven to 180°C

Firstly, cook the sweet potatoes by placing them on a baking tray. Season with salt and black pepper, add thyme and bay leaf. Drizzle with olive oil and cover the baking tray with foil. Cook for 15-20mins until fully cooked.

To prepare the seabass, place a non-stick pan over medium flame with olive oil and add leek, mushroom, basil. Season with salt and pepper. Stir fry them for 4-5 mins.

Now add vermouth and wine and simmer for two mins over a high flame until reduced by half. Rinse, dry the fidh then season with salt and pepper.. Lower the heat and place the fish with the skin sie down.

Cook for 8 mins with a lid on and add the butter and stir. The fish is cooked when the flesh turns white and flakes easily.

To serve, put the sweet potatoes slices onto warmed plates, then place the fish on top uisng a fish spatula and pour over the sauce and vegetables

**Simon Morris
Buoy and Oyster**

Cooking should be well thought out, simple, enjoyable but more importantly, tasty to eat.

Plan - what your going to cook, discover the best way to execute that dish.
Simple - stick with a style or theme and don't blend too many flavours.
Enjoyable - enjoy buying new ingredients and trying fresh & different cuts.
Tasty - Big Bold Flavours every time.

I always think it's best to start with buying the best protein you can afford, whether that's fresh daily caught Dover Sole from your fishmonger or aged ribeye steak from your butcher. Work from there, looking at what vegetables are seasonally grown and what's locally available. Pairing it with a good sauce, oil, dressing that packs a punch.

Simon Morris - Buoy and Oyster

SKATE WING

Also known as Thornback Ray, skate is a very sustainable species and in abundance in our waters. It can be tricky to skin, so ask your fishmonger to do this for you

Ingredients

Local skate wings
2 large skate wing
Oil
Butter
Parchment paper
Lemon

Brown shrimp, caper & seaweed
100g brown shrimp
50g lilliput capers
20g edible seaweed
50g samphire
30g salty fingers/monks beard
50ml white wine
100g cold unsalted butter

"There is a slightly larger side so we recommend shallow frying this side first"

Method

Put the white wine into a saucepan and bring to a simmer. Slowly add the cold butter to create a buttery white wine emulsion.

Add the brown shrimps and slowly stir but don't boil, just keep warm. Add the chopped edible seaweed.

Add the blanched samphire and salty fingers. Finish by adding the lilliput capers, keep warm and keep stirring. It is very important you don't boil or it will split

Bring the dish together. In a fish pan put oil and parchment bring to the heat. Add the seasoned skate wing, slowly cook until a nice golden colour. Turn over and add the half lemon to the pan.

Roast in an oven at 180°C for 12-14 mins, or until you can pull the top bone knuckle away from the wing. Once cooked allow it to rest.

Place on the plate with the seared burnt lemon and top with pre-made brown shrimp and caper butter.

RYE BAY SCALLOPS
Mango and coconut cream, pickled radish, burnt leek and shoots

With scallops you get what you pay for! Keep an eye open for scallops in their shell; the larger the better

Ingredients

Scallops
12 scallops
Oil
Butter
Mango and coconut cream
1 bag frozen mango pieces
2 small tins coconut milk
50ml vegetable oil
1 tsp cumin
1 tsp paprika
1 tsp cayenne pepper
1 tsp chilli garlic purée
2 diced onions
100ml fish stock
100ml white wine
Salt and pepper for seasoning

Pickled radish
200g mooli radish
100ml white wine vinegar
100g caster sugar
Aromats
1 star anise
1 cinnamon stick
3 cloves
1 bay leaf

Burnt leek
1 whole leek

Garnish
Fresh red English radish in water.
Shots, ideally coriander cress but
tendril pea shoots work

Serves 4

For best results it's important to use a very hot, lightly oiled, non-stick pan. I keep the roe on the scallop but this is a personal preference. Remember that you must trim off the small connective tissue

Method

Sweat the diced onions, garlic and chilli paste down in a deep-bottomed pan in a little oil, add the dry spice and allow the spices to cook to release their flavours. Add the diced mango, fry with the other ingredients. Deglaze the pan with the white wine and fish stock. Add the coconut milk and allow to simmer until the mango is tender.

Once tender, put the mix in a blender and blitz. Once blitzed put it all in the same pan and season to your taste with salt and pepper. This can be made in advance, possibly the day before to allow the spices and flavours to infuse.

To make the radish, bring the vinegar and sugar to the boil with the aromats. Slice the mooli on a mandolin, or really thin with a knife. Allow liquor to cool slightly and pour over the radish. Again, this can be done the day before to allow to pickle.

Take the white of the leek and dice. Place on an oven tray and roast until black and crunchy. Once burnt allow to cool and place into a blender and blitz to a fine dust.

Bringing the dish together, in a hot pan add a little oil, place the scallops down and sear the scallops either side with a nice golden colour. Once turned, add a knob of butter and set aside to rest.

In a saucepan heat a small amount of the sauce and bring to a simmer. Place the sauce in the bowl. Place the rested scallops on top of the sauce.

Garnish with pickled mooli and fresh radish. Dust with burnt leek. Place coriander, cress or fresh tendril pea shoots on top.

Rob Taylor
Compasses Inn

Inn

"*At The Compasses we like to keep the food simple while using the best ingredients we can buy. I feel if you start with really good foundations then half the work is done for you in producing delicious food. As a chef I write menus that I hope will make customers smile. I often use classic flavours and ingredients people are comfortable with.*"

Rob Taylor - Compasses Inn

SALMON
Salmon with cucumber and oyster

The Compasses is a pub foremost. So our main dishes need to be substantial enough for diners looking for a bite to eat on their way home but at the same time take into account those diners looking for three courses. Consequently a lot of our starters at the pub tend to be lighter, such as the following salmon dish for example. The dish is light but bursting with flavours. Just enough to get all your taste buds going for the rest of the meal to follow

Ingredients

Smoked salmon
1 side of salmon
300g coarse sea salt
150g sugar I prefer to use dark muscavado
1 bunch of dill

Cucumber pickle
1 cucumber
1tsp of mixed corriander seeds, black pepper corns and fennel seeds
75ml of white wine vinegar
3g of xantham gum
Seasoning

Oyster emulsion
4 oysters
1g agar
100ml pomace olive oil
Seasoning
5ml malt vinegar

> *I added the oyster to this dish because it added a nice little salty bite, although it's very subtle. I always feel it's very important have a variety of flavours going on in a dish*

Method

Smoked Salmon. Wash the salmon and remove any pin bones.

Mix all the other ingredients together and cover the salmon, turn over and repeat. Place the salmon in the fridge overnight for the cure to work. Remove from fridge and wash the cure off patting the salmon down with a clean cloth.

Cucumber pickle. Dice 1 whole cucumber and place in a blender with all the other ingredients. Blend until slightly chopped but not smooth. Then place in fine strainer and leave to hang over night, discard the liquid and the remaining pulp is the cucumber pickle you will use.

Oyster emulsion. Start by gently simmering the oysters in their shell for 10 mins, once cool remove from the shell and place in a blender, add all other ingredients and blend until smooth and creamy.

PIGEON
Black pudding ball, potato terrine and quince chutney

This dish came together just from finding the main components close to the pub. For example, the pigeons are shot on a local game estate and the quinces delivered by a local resident from his own garden

Ingredients

1 oven ready pigeon

Quince chutney
1.5kg quince
2 onions
370 brown sugar
300ml vinegar
2 chillis
100 ginger
2 star anise
1tsp corriandor seed

Red wine jus
50g of vegetable oil
2 shallots
2 garlic cloves
2 flat mushrooms
200ml port
4 sprigs of thyme
200 ml chicken stock
300ml veal stock
50g redcurrant jelly

Black pudding ball
200g of the best black pudding
2 eggs
100g flour
100g breadcrumbs

Potato terrine
10 Maris Piper
250g pancetta
75g butter
Potato starch
Salt and pepper

Red cabbage
1kg sliced red cabbage
400g sliced red onions
400g sliced bramley apple
1 clove of garlic
¼ grated nutmeg
¼ teaspoon of ground cinnamon
¼ teaspoon of cloves
300g light muscovado sugar
200g redcurrant jelly
30ml red wine vinegar
20g butter

> *When I put a dish together featuring game for example, which packs more flavour, I like to couple it with a bit of sweetness. Hence the quince and red cabbage. The flavours of this dish scream autumn, which is also my favourite season as a chef who loves to cook bold, comforting food*

Method

Quince Chutney. Sweat down the onions. slowly. Once tender add the remaining ingredients and cook out until sticky and the quince is tender.

Red wine jus. Heat the oil in a pan and add the sliced shallots, garlic, mushrooms, and thyme. Pan fry until golden and deglaze the pan with port. Once this has reduced a little add the stock and reduce, skimming the fat from the top. Once reduced by half finish with redcurrant jelly and strain through a sieve

Black pudding ball. Remove black pudding from any skin and place in a bowl, break down and add one egg. Mix until smooth and roll into balls (I used one about the size of a ping pong ball). Once rolled, coat in flour and shake off any excess. Continue this process with the remaining egg then the breadcrumbs. Once completely covered, deep fry at 180°C until golden.

Potato terrine. Start by washing, peeling and slicing the potatoes as finely as possible using a mandolin. Once sliced place in a bowl and mix with the melted butter, seasoning and two teaspoons of potato starch. Place one layer of potatoes in the bottom and then layer with pancetta. Continue this process until all potatoes have been used. Place on a tray in a pre-heated oven at 180°C for around an hour or until a knife can pass through the slices with no resistance. Press the potatoes overnight then de-mould and portion as required.

Red cabbage. First discard the tough outer leaves of the cabbage, cut it into quarters and remove the hard stalk. Then shred the rest of the cabbage finely, using your sharpest knife (you can shred it in a food processor). Next, in a fairly large casserole, arrange a layer of shredded cabbage seasoned with salt and pepper, then a layer of chopped onions and apples with a sprinkling of the garlic, spices and sugar. Continue with these alternate layers until everything is in. Now pour in the wine vinegar and lastly add dots of butter on the top.

Put a tight lid on the casserole and let it cook very slowly in the oven for 2-2½ hours, stirring everything around once or twice during the cooking. Once cooked, the red cabbage will keep warm without coming to any harm, and it will also reheat very successfully.

Matt Sworder
The Corner House

My ethos is to put The Corner House at the heart of the community, showcasing the best of Kentish produce. Dishes cooked by people with skill and passion; simple dishes with great flavours, served by people determined to deliver a great guest experience.

The guiding principles in our restaurants is that we source the best local produce and deliver great tasting food at a sensible price. The guest is at the heart of everything we do. That's a philosophy that's earned us a loyal following.

Matt Sworder - Corner House

NEW CHURCH LAMB SHOULDER, LOW AND SLOW
Saffron Velouté

If there is one dish that has helped build the reputation of the restaurants, it would be this. It's our top-selling sharing dish and it provides real theatre at the table. It's not so much carved at the table as pulled apart, because it just falls off the bone. It gives us chefs a chance to come into the dining room and serve it, or allow our front-of-house team quality time with the guests, as they explain how it has been cooked

Ingredients

1 whole lamb shoulder
2 onions, rough dice
2 carrots, rough dice
2 sticks celery, rough dice
1 bulb of garlic
½ bunch rosemary
½ bunch thyme
1 bottle red wine
2 litre lamb stock
Salt and pepper

A real dinner party centrepiece and one I would urge you to try at home

Method

Set the oven to 150°C.

In a large baking tray, sear the lamb shoulder in a little vegetable oil until it is beautifully golden brown all over.
Making sure the meat is golden brown is a really important step, as that helps to start rendering the fat and caramelising the natural sugars in the meat.

Add the vegetables into the baking tray and cover immediately with the red wine, herbs and the lamb stock. Cover with foil and place in the oven for four hours.

Meanwhile, make the dauphinoise potatoes according to your favourite recipe.

After four hours, ensure the lamb is falling off the bone, and set aside. Strain the lamb stock through the sieve, ensuring all the flavour from the pulp of the vegetables is extracted.

Reduce by two thirds for the lamb jus. Pass the lamb jus through a fine sieve.

Ideally, you should use a muslin cloth if you have one, or a new J-cloth if not. Taste, adjusting the seasoning as necessary.

Place the whole lamb shoulder on a serving board, add a little jus over the lamb and serve with dauphinoise potatoes, seasonal vegetables and lamb jus.

STICKY DATE SPONGE PUDDING
With Gadds No 5

This delicious dessert is evocative of a sticky toffee pudding, although we cunningly slip in a little Kentish beer to help things along. Gadds' No 5 Ale is the secret ingredient in this dessert and it makes all the difference

Ingredients

Sponge
100g butter
200g brown sugar
2 tbsp treacle
2 eggs
200g self-raising flour
275ml water
200g chopped dates
1 tbsp bicarbonate of soda

Salted caramel sauce
37.5g best quality unsalted butter
25g soft light brown sugar
25g caster sugar
25g golden syrup
62.5ml double cream
⅓ tsp Maldon sea salt

Make sure you use the best quality dates that you can find and keep testing your caramel sauce when you add the salt, so that you use just the right amount

Method

Bring the water to the boil with the dates and bicarbonate of soda until thick.

During that time, beat the butter and sugar together. Add the eggs, treacle and dates. Fold in the flour.

Bake in a baking tray at 170°C for 40-45 mins. Remove from the oven and rest for 5 mins.

Prick with a cocktail stick and then soak the sponge in 300ml Gadds No.5 Ale.

Serve warm with hot salted caramel sauce and ice cream.

Fish on the

Peter Baldwin
Fish on the Green

Green

"*Working in service kitchens and on fish sections my whole career I have always leaned towards the "Hot side" of the kitchen. Fish preparation and cookery is an exact skill requiring precision handling and timing. It is also in most cases a last-minute, cook to order ingredient leading to a fast-paced and exciting service. Having built a great team of chefs over the last ten years, who share the same passion for cooking as I do, makes Fish on the Green a great place to work.*

I am in a sense a simple chef who likes to keep things simple. I find that this is for me the best form of cookery. When menus are kept simple they are easier to teach, better for consistency and at the same time appeal to a wider customer base. Essentially, simple but done well, is my cooking philosophy ....

SCALLOPS WITH PORK BELLY
Roast onion pureé

Scallops are widely available all year round but are at their best in the Winter months between October and March. They are a favourite on any menu and cooked and seasoned correctly are unrivalled in flavour and appetising appearance

Ingredients

12 scallops (3 each)
1 x large white onion
50g butter
100ml milk
100ml double cream
Pork belly
Rock salt
Thyme
Garlic
Pork fat
Chives
Rapeseed oil

Serves 4

" Treat the scallop with care when cooking. Season well and sear the scallops lighty for 30 seconds to a minute in a hot pan taking care not to over cook. Then simply season with rock salt and lemon to really bring out the flavour "

Method

Prize open the scallops, clean and dry well, season. Pan fry on a medium heat until lightly caramelised but do not overcook. Finish with rock salt and lemon juice

For the onion pureé, dice onions and fry gently in a pan on a low heat in butter until browned. Cover with equal amounts of milk and double cream and cook until soft. Pureé the sauce, pass through a sieve and season.

Salt the pork belly overnight with the rock salt, garlic and thyme. Wash off the marinade and place in a roasting tray. Cover with pork fat and bring up to heat in the oven at 225°C, cover and cook at 100°C for around four to five hours depending on size.

Lift from the fat and pick the meat off, season and roll into a sausage shape in cling film. Slice into pieces and pan fry a slice when cooking the scallops.

For the chive oil, blend chives and rapeseed oil until smooth, pass through a sieve and keep in the fridge.

JOHN DORY WITH CRUSHED POTATOES
Saffron Veloute

John Dory is a great locally caught, salt water, Kentish fish. A fish that most fisherman are happy to see in their nets as it demands a high price at market. Also known as Saint Pierre, its markings either side are said to depict the finger marks of Saint Peter, where he picked it from the ocean. It's also unique having six fillets, with three on either side. It's a real customer and chefs' favourite with its buttery taste and firm and flaky in texture. When scored well and cooked correctly John Dory is easily one of the greats. Whatever it's paired with on our menu it never fails to be a bestseller

Ingredients

Fillets of John Dory
New potatoes
Mussels
Bunch of asparagus
Spring onions
Chopped parsley

Equal quantities of:-
Fish stock
White wine
Double cream

Crushed potatoes x 4-6 people
500g of cooked and peeled new
potatoes (we use locally grown
Nichola potatoes)
30ml of extra virgin olive oil
Good squeeze of lemon juice
seasoning

Saffron velouté x 4-6 people
200ml white wine
200ml fish stock
200ml double cream
pinch of saffron strands
20-30 cooked mussels
12 asparagus spears
3 finely sliced spring onions
¼ bunch of chopped parsley

"With this recipe it's essential when cooking the John Dory to crisp the skin. Ensure the skin is well scored using a sharp knife by making long and fine incisions from top to bottom of the fillet. Doing this will stop the skin from curling once it hits the heat allowing the fish to stay in full contact with the pan. Once the skin is crisp and golden brown carefully turn the fillet, remove the pan from the heat and leave the fish in the pan for a minute, allowing the residual heat to finish it off"

Method

Cook and peel your new potatoes and then crush with extra virgin olive oil and season well.

Make the saffron velouté by placing the fish stock in a pan and reducing by half. Add the white wine and reduce by half again, adding a pinch of saffron at the end. Add the cream and reduce to a sauce consistency
Finish the sauce with steamed mussels, blanched asparagus, sliced spring onions, chopped parsley and seasoning.

While making the sauce, score the John Dory skin and season on both sides. Pan fry skin side down on a medium heat for one to two mins. When the skin is crisp turn the fish over and remove from the heat.

Plate the crushed potato on the plate, spoon over the saffron velouté and place the John Dory on top.

David Hart
Folkestone Wine Company

Folkestone Wi

"Seasonality and simplicity are the two key factors in my cooking. Working with the seasons gives you each ingredient at its peak and somehow nature seems to provide the best flavour combinations too. Think asparagus, wild garlic and morels, gooseberries and elderflower or sweetcorn and girolles. Using each ingredient at it's best, then moving onto the next seasonal delight is all the inspiration a chef could ask for and in Kent we are blessed with some of the UK's best.

When working with such fantastic produce it's only common sense to allow the diner to focus on the quality of each component of the dish and the harmony of the flavours. In short- keep it simple...

PICKLED HERRING
Kohlrabi and Apple

I love the fresh clean flavours of this dish. The aniseed notes of the fennel and dill work well with the oil-rich herring, as does the crunch and turnip-like quality of the kohlrabi which also lends depth. The buttermilk rounds everything out. A most harmonious plate

Ingredients

8 pickled herrings
2 kohlrabi
2 apples
Tablespoon buttermilk
Juice of ½ organic lemon
Pinch of salt
White pepper
Tablespoon chopped fennel or dill

Use the freshest, most crisp apples and kohlrabi you can find

Method

If you don't have buttermilk, plain natural yogurt will do just fine.

Take eight pickled herring fillets and slice each fillet neatly in half.

Peel two kohlrabi and slice into a bowl using a mandolin. Slice two apples in the same way, stopping short of the core. Add a tablespoon of buttermilk and the juice of half a lemon to the kholrabi mix along with a pinch of salt, white pepper and a tablespoon of chopped fennel fronds (reserve a few sprigs for decoration, use dill if fennel is unavailable).

Mix well.

To assemble, place a spoonful of the kohlrabi mixture onto the plate, then half a herring fillet, then another spoon of kohlrabi and so on until each plate has four pieces of herring. The idea being that each mouthful has a bit of everything. Finish with a turn of white pepper and a few fennel fronds for decoration.

Folkestone Wine
Company

CHOCOLATE MARQUIS
Ottinge Farm cream and ginger caramel

This recipe is based on the chocolate marquise served at Le Taillevant restaurant in Paris, a temple of old-school gastronomy. Admittedly not very Kentish so far. However, what makes this dessert is the wonderful, unctuous unpasterised cream made on Ottinge Farm, conveniently just down the road from us in Folkestone

Ingredients

Chocolate Marquis
275g unsalted butter
420g dark chocolate
8 medium eggs
150g icing sugar

Ginger caramel
250g sugar
Handful of ginger

Ottinge Farm cream

Use the best chocolate you can afford, Valrhona is a good choice. I can't think of a better wine to accompany this than a fine glass of Madeira

Method

Have ready 275g unsalted butter at room temperature. Weigh out 420g of dark chocolate in a heatproof bowl and gently melt over a pan of simmering water. Separate 8 medium eggs into two bowls. Weigh out 150g of icing sugar and pass through a sieve. Once the chocolate has fully melted add two thirds of the icing sugar to the chocolate and stir until dissolved. Now add the butter, stirring occasionally until you have a smooth homogenous mass. Take the bowl of chocolate mixture off the heat and allow to cool.

Meanwhile, line a terrine with cling film allowing an overlap to cover. Whisk the egg whites in a scrupulously clean bowl with a pinch of salt until you achieve soft peaks, now whisk in the remaining icing sugar until you have firm peaks. Once the chocolate is down to body temperature stir in the egg yolks one by one. Add one third of the egg whites and beat into the chocolate mixture thoroughly. Now using a large spoon, fold the remaining egg whites into the mix retaining as much air as possible. Once smooth and streak-free decant the mixture into your awaiting cling-film lined receptacle, cover with cling-film and chill for at least six hours.

For the caramel, weigh out 250g sugar in a medium sized heavy based saucepan. Add water to just cover, and heat over a medium flame. Meanwhile, grate a whole hand of ginger onto a plate. When the caramel is the colour of a conker and the first whisps of smoke are showing switch off the heat and add the ginger (be careful as it will splutter). Stir with a wooden spoon, and leave to infuse for 20 mins. Pass through a fine sieve.

To serve, cut finger-thick slices using a warm knife (hold the knife under hot water for a few seconds), dust with cocoa powder and transfer to a plate. Surround with a tablespoon of ginger caramel and top with a generous spoonful of Ottinge Farm cream.

Fordwich A

Fordwich Arms

Dan Smith
Fordwich Arms

Arms

"*Our food at The Fordwich Arms is entirely seasonal, if its not in season we will not use it which can be quite restricting, but does ensure the produce is always of the best quality. Working with local suppliers allows us to plan our menus ahead and be able to develop and test ideas. When the ingredients are in their prime we are ready to start using them. We do not restrict ourselves by using entirely local produce but we are very fortunate to be in a location such as Kent where we can get phenomenal seafood from the coast, the best quality fruit and vegetables and superior meat and game. With produce this good it is important not to over complicate things and really let the produce speak for itself.*

Being a relatively new restaurant we are still adapting and improving things everyday. As a restaurant it is important to develop and continually try and improve what you do, having said that it is also important to keep the standards

CHART FARM SILKA VENISON
Celeriac, damson and smoked bone marrow

The venison dish is a real celebration of autumn. I love the combination of meat and fruit which is an age-old classic. The sharpness of the damson really helps to cut through the richness of the meat and the smoked bone marrow. The venison from Chart Farm really is the best quality, they take a lot of care in what they do and it really shows

Ingredients

500g Venison loin trimmed

Sauce
1litre brown chicken stock
2 carrots
2 shallots
6 sprigs thyme
200g venison trim

Celeriac pureé
400g diced celeriac
150g milk
50g cream
10g salt

Baked celeriac
1 celeriac peeled and cut into 8ths
8 sprigs thyme
rapeseed oil
sea salt

Damson pureé
200g damsons stones removed
100g sugar
50g water

Brussel sprout leaves
100g brussels
15g butter
salt

Smoked bone marrow
2 marrow bones 4 inches long cut vertically
Hay

In any dish the protein is always the most important element

Method

For the venison, trim the saddle of any sinew and portion into 120g pieces. Remove from the fridge 30 mins before cooking to bring the meat to room temperature. To cook, season all over with salt and pepper and seal in a very hot pan with some oil for about 30 seconds on each side. Add a knob of butter, a sprig of thyme, a cracked garlic clove and roast in a 180°C oven for one minute then turn and roast for one more minute on the other side. Remove from the oven and baste with the butter for 30 seconds. Remove from the pan and rest with the butter over the top for two mins. Carve each piece into two and sprinkle with sea salt.

For the pureé, cook the celeriac in the milk, cream and salt until tender then blend until smooth.

For the damson pureé, mix the sugar and water and bring to the boil for two mins. You will see the water will seem to become a bit thicker as it boils, then add the fruit and cook for five mins. Blend until smooth.

For the baked celeriac, peel a medium sized celeriac and cut into half and then each half cut into 4. Wrap each piece in tin foil with some sea salt, rapeseed oil and a sprig of thyme. Bake for 10-12 mins at 180°C, check by poking a cocktail stick into the centre. It should have a little resistance but not be completely firm.

For the smoked bone marrow, ask your butcher to cut it through the bone lengthways to reveal the marrow. Place some hay in the bottom of a saucepan before placing the bones with the marrow upright in order to protect it and stop it from melting. Set fire to the hay and place a lid on the pan to cut the flames and start the smoke. Leave to sit for five mins then scrape the marrow from the bones and dice.

For the sauce, fry the venison trim in a pan with a small amount of oil until golden all over, then add the chopped carrot, shallot and thyme and cook for five mins. Add the chicken stock, bring to a simmer and cook for one hour reducing slowly, season to taste. Once the sauce has thickened, pass through a fine sieve and at the last minute add the chopped bone marrow or it will completely melt into the sauce.

For the brussel sprout leaves, cut the base of each sprout and remove each leaf one at a time and place into ice water, this will help to firm up the leaves and freshen them. Boil 100ml water with 50g butter and drop the leaves in for 15 seconds. Quickly remove them and plate immediately.

PUMPKIN PIE
Latte Chantilly

Pumpkin pie is one of my childhood memories of one of my first holidays to America, so I'm creating a bit of nostalgia

Ingredients

Sweet pastry
500g butter
350g icing sugar sifter
5 eggs
1 pinch salt
zest of 1 orange
1kg plain flour

Pumpkin pie mix
2 eggs
1 egg yolk
500g pumpkin puree
170g evaporated milk
140g dark brown sugar
2tsp ginger syrup
2tsp ground cinnamon
½tsp ground ginger
½ nutmeg grated
Half vanilla pod

Latte Chantilly
600g double cream
200g caster sugar
10g espresso
2 bronze gelatine leaves

Stem ginger ice cream
1 litre whole milk
200g egg yolk
150g caster sugar
2 whole stem gingers grated
200g double cream

Nougatine tuille
500g caster sugar
200g pumpkin seeds

> *Pre-heat the oven and make the sweet paste the day before*

Method

For the sweet pastry, cream the butter and sugar, add the flour, orange and salt, add the eggs little by little to bind. Portion into blocks and refrigerate. Once this is done whisk the pumpkin pie mix together and set aside.

To make the latte Chantilly, boil cream with sugar and espresso. Add the soaked gelatine and refrigerate overnight. The next day whisk up until light and fluffy. Put in a piping bag with a star nozzle ready to use.

Now for the stem ginger ice cream. Boil the milk with the stem ginger. Whisk the egg yolks with the sugar, and pour into the milk, whisk this to 82°C and then cool down over ice. Add cold cream and churn in an ice cream churner.

For the nougartine tuille, make a dry caramel by cooking the sugar in a pan until dark and glossy. Add the pumpkin seeds and pour onto a tray. When set, blitz to a fine crumb.

To make the tuilles, you need a silpat baking mat and a ring the size of the tart shell you are using and a sieve. Sieve the nougatine onto the silpat over the ring cutter then remove and repeat to get perfect round circles. Bake at 180°C for about eight mins until golden and cooked.

To assemble the tart roll your sweet pastry and line your tart cases, refrigerate until the pastry is cool. Blind bake the tart shells, at about 160°C until golden brown, brush with egg yolk and bake again.

Pour in the pumpkin pie mix, turn the oven down to 150°C and depending on the size of your tart bake them. Mine were small so took about 15 mins, you can tell when they are cooked as the top will no longer be gooey. Let them cool.

To assemble the dessert, place the tart in the middle of plate, pipe three dots of latte Chantilly, decorate either sides of the Chantilly with edible flowers, cresses and gold leaf.

Roche your ice cream in the middle of the 3 dots and then place your nougatine tuille on top of the ice cream.

GB Pizza

We cook our marinara (tomato) sauce long and slow, for at least three hours. To make it at home, fry off onions and garlic until browned. Add good quality tinned tomatoes, a pinch of unrefined caster sugar, salt and a squeeze of lemon juice and cook down very gently.

Our Crab Pizza is a summer best-seller. We get our crab meat from Broadstairs' amazing fishmonger: Fruits de Mer.
You can now buy pretty decent, ready-made pizza dough from the chiller cabinet at the supermarket, but it always tastes better when you make your own. Heat your oven as high as it will go, and put a baking sheet inside. This needs to get good and hot, too. Roll out the dough as thin as it goes and shape into a circle, pushing the dough out from the middle.
Add a ladle of your homemade tomato sauce, and then the rest of the toppings.

55g home-made tomato sauce	25g shredded Mozzarella
10 sprigs of samphire	10 slices of red chilli
2 dessert spoons of fresh crab meat (evenly scattered)	

Give the pizza a good squeeze of fresh lemon juice after cooking, and add some dressed rocket leaves, if you fancy some greenery.

GB Pizza Co

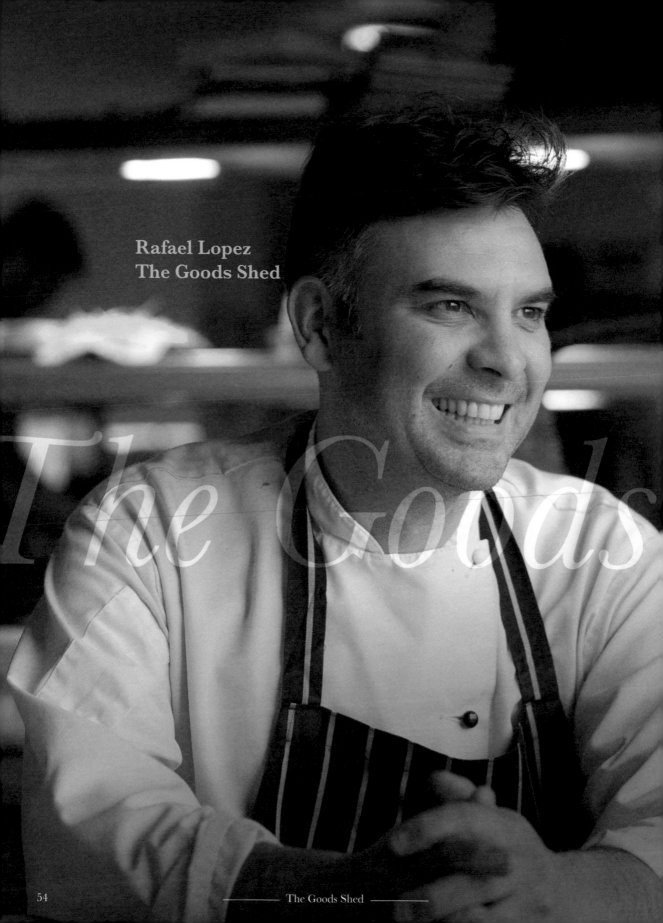

Rafael Lopez
The Goods Shed

Shed

"In the kitchen we all wear our apron up. Like Marco Pierre-White once said… 'We are all commis chefs!' I might know more about food than a lot of people and no doubt others know more but I am always curious and interested…always learning.

Over the years we have built strong relationships with producers, farmers, fishmongers and foragers. Our food is as local as possible and always seasonal. If an item on the menu is not in season it's because we've pickled it, cured it, fermented it, preserved it or dried it. Otherwise freshness is our key. To take an example some vegetables don't even go near a fridge. They are picked at 6am, delivered to us within two hours, then washed and prepared, ready for lunch or dinner enabling us to respect their natural sweetness.

But my approach to cooking is a "productionist". We like to treat a humble onion like a valuable truffle. Every season we pick certain produce and we try to develop original ways of extracting flavour. It's a continual learning curve using a lot of creativity and continual assessment. Sometimes what didn't work in one way works in another."

Rafael Lopez - The Goods Shed

MALLARD, BEETROOT AND BLACKBERRIES

The mallard is a small wild duck available as the game season starts in September. The flesh is deep, grassy, sweet and delicate. From an active life the bird is virtually fat free, so cooking it on the bone is a must

Ingredients

1 mallard duck
Beetroot
Blackberries
Seasonal greens

Our approach to meat, fish and poultry is nose to tail. I'm naturally economical with our produce, respecting the produce and the labour involved bringing it to us. I don't like waste

Method

The jointed legs are braised slowly with herbs such as thyme and rosemary, while red wine helps deepen the flavour. The addition of carrot and onions will soften the flavours and give good body to the sauce. (30-40 min should do depending on quantity of liquid and speed of simmering).

Then the crown of the bird is fried in a hot pan to extract the roasted bone flavour and at the same time maintaining the shape of the breast (it should take no more than 10-15 min depending on the fierceness of the heat). When cooked the breast meat near the wishbone should give slightly. When the crown is cool to the touch the meat will be perfectly rested and the breast carved off the bone.

September is also a great month for rooty, earthy beetroot and sweet, sharp blackberries. The pairing of purples makes a fantastic visual dish.

We make a chocolate vinegar with 70% dark chocolate, balsamic vinegar and a little sugar.

I'll leave the rest to your imagination.

SLIP SOLE
Nasturtium butter

Smaller Dover Sole known as slip sole have flesh which is white, dense and almost sweet. They are widely available from about April. Get your fishmonger to skin both sides to let your flavours penetrate the flesh better.

Nasturtium is a edible garden plant, which comes in a variety of colours...yellows, oranges, reds. It's got a subtle peppery taste. We combine the chopped flowers and stems (and even the buds towards the end of the season) with some sautéed shallots, the zest of a lemon and some unsalted butter. All mixed together this is rolled into a cylinder and cooled in the fridge.

The sole is best grilled. Season the tray with a little oil and salt and place the slip sole on it. Lightly season with salt and place cut disc of the nasturtium butter on top. Grill on a hot setting for about two mins, then baste the fish with the melted butter and cook for a further two mins. Serve the fish with another disc of butter on top and some fresh nasturtium flowers of your choice.

An elegant dish to enjoy in one of those warm early summer lunches.

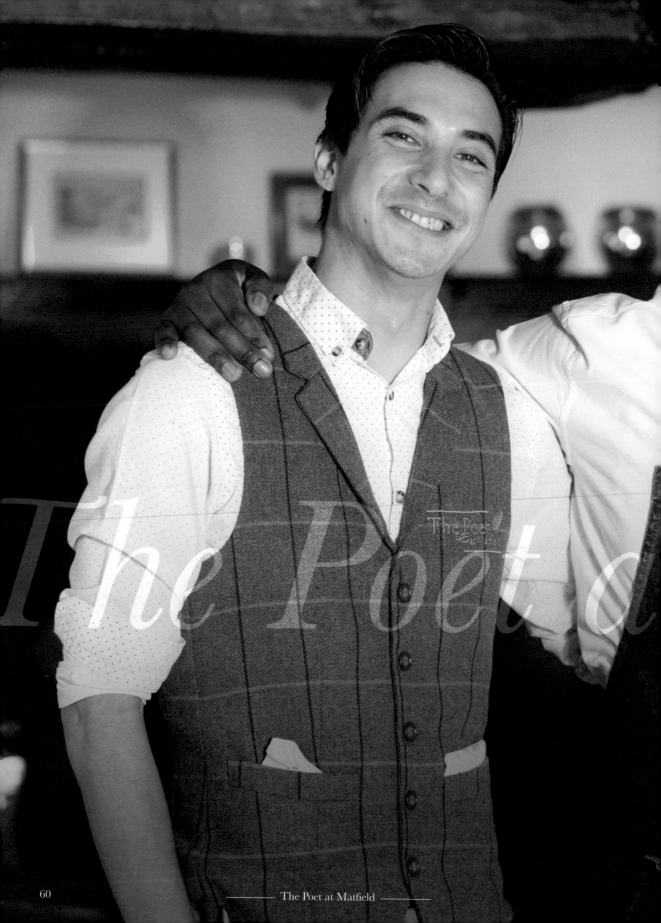

Petrus Madutela
The Poet at Matfield

The Poet
at Matfield

"
When I was growing up in the township of Mothotlung in South Africa, my mum used to serve simple food, cooked with love and care. She'd boil chicken with salt and a serving of pap, the maize based porridge that's a South African staple. I can still remember the flavours and that was a great lesson for me. The best food is natural, simple and full of taste. It's about bringing people together around a table and sharing.

My passion for cooking developed when I took a job as a kitchen porter at Pecanwood Golf & Country Estate, near Pretoria. I was always asking the chefs lots of questions and eventually they asked me to join them. I jumped at the opportunity. I learnt by buying chef books and magazines and by comparing different ways of transforming dishes and presenting food. Even now I still immerse myself in books, while the internet is a great source of inspiration. I'll never stop learning.
"

Petrus Madutela - The Poet at Matfield

ROASTED LOCAL QUAIL BALLONTINE
Confit leg, mushroom duxelle with a Sherry sauce

Game birds are in abundance around October and quail has remained my favourite. It's a delicious bird with some wonderful characteristics; it is juicy with a wide flavour profile and not too gamey

Ingredients

4 quail plugged and cleaned
50g butter
200ml duck fat
Sprig of thyme
2 clove of garlic

Duxelle

200g button mushroom diced finely
1 clove garlic creamed
1 banana shallot diced finely
10ml sherry
5ml truffle oil
Salt and pepper to taste
50ml double cream

Sauce

2 banana shallot diced
2 prig of thyme
1 clove garlic
300l beef stock (buy from the supermarket)
20ml of sherry
50ml good cooking red wine

Serves 4

Take the quails out of the fridge about an hour before cooking and pat them dry inside and out with paper a towel.

Take care not to overcook the quail, as it can easily become dry and tough. It's cooked when the meat is slightly firm to touch, and juices run clear. The meat should be slightly pink

Method

To prepare the quail, with a sharp knife remove the legs and be careful not to damage the skin.

For the confit legs, put the duck fat, garlic and thyme in a small pan. Once the fat is melted add the leg and poach at low heat. This will take approximately 25 mins. Once cooked take them out of the liquid and rest.

For the ballontine, debone the rest of the bird. Start from the back working with the tip of your knife as close to the bone as possible. Season the deboned quail with salt and pepper, and put on top of tin foil with a nob of butter and roll into a cylinder. Secure the ends tightly. In hot pan add some oil and seal the sides for two mins.

Pre-heat the oven to 180°C and roast the quail for six mins, then let it rest.

For the sauce, in a pan fry the carcasses, onion, garlic and thyme from the quail until golden brown. Add the red wine and stock and reduce by one third, strain with a very fine sieve Add sherry to the strained sauce and bring to boil for two mins.

For the duxelle, in a pan add butter and sweat the onion and garlic for 6 mins. Add the mushroom and cook until dry. Add the cream, reduce and season to taste. Finish with truffle oil.

Marcin Szelka
Rocksalt

"
I was born in Cracow, Southern Poland. My cooking career started when I was teenager cooking for my family. I then joined a five year programme in chef's college where I could further my knowledge about gastronomy. I came to England after college to learn how to cook with some of the best chefs in the country. I worked for Gordon Ramsey at Claridge's for a few years before moving to Folkestone, where I joined Mark Sergeant's team in his brand new restaurant Rocksalt. I started off as a senior chef de partie before my appointment to the top spot of Head Chef. It's a position which I am proud to have held for the past three years.
"

Marcin Szelka - Rocksalt

PLAICE, BEURRE BLANC AND GREEN SAUCE

This is a very simple dish, which is full of flavour using fantastic local fish from the east Kent coast. Sweet flat fish balanced well with a rich butter sauce, fresh herbs and peppery watercress gives the perfect finish to the dish

Ingredients

4 whole plaice 450-550g (ask your fishmonger to skin the fish on both sides as the skin can be soggy and not so appealing for consumption)
1 lemon wedged into four
200g fresh watercress

Beurre blanc
(Reduction)
25g butter
2 shallots sliced
15g pepper corns
250ml white wine vinegar
250ml white wine

(Finishing)
50ml fish stock
1tsp cream
150g unsalted butter

Green Sauce
½ bunch of mint leaves
½ bunch parsley leaves
½ bunch green basil
40g large capers
10g salted anchovies
1 clove of garlic, peeled and crushed
200ml rapeseed oil
Seasoning

Serves 4

Pre heat the oven to 200°C (grilled option would be perfect). Rub the fish with a little rapeseed or olive oil and season with salt and pepper. Grill for about 10 mins (flesh side up) depending on the size of the fish. Mix the green sauce and the beurre blanc (butter sauce) together and smother the fish with it. Serve with lemon and watercress

Method

First make the beurre blanc reduction by sweating the shallots in butter until soft. Add the peppercorns and vinegar and reduce by half. Add the white wine and reduce again by half. Strain using a fine sieve

Finish the sauce by bringing the reduction and fish stock to the boil and reduce by a third. Add the cream and then gradually whisk in the butter to form an emulsion. Season with salt & pepper. Don't boil or the butter will split out.

For the green sauce finely chop all the herbs with a sharp knife making only 2 cuts so they do not bruise or blacken. Finely chop the capers, anchovies and garlic and mix with the herbs. Slowly add the rapeseed oil to bind the mixture. Be careful not to make the sauce too oily. It may not need all of the rapeseed oil so use your judegement.

Add to the beurre blanc according to taste and season.

GYPSY TART

Gypsy tart is a classic Kentish dessert which is now to be found nationwide. Approximately 100 years ago it was originally made by a Kent lady with very limited ingredients, who needed to feed undernourished gypsy kids playing outside her house

Ingredients

Gypsy tart
410g evaporated milk (1 can)
340g Muscavado sugar
1x 25cm x 4cm blind baked tart case

Lemon cream
500ml double cream
50g icing sugar
Zest and juice from 1 lemon

To make a small tart just divide both ingredients by half

Sweet pastry case
250g soft flour
125g butter
125g icing sugar
1 Eggs
Seeds of one vanilla pod
Pinch of salt

" Make sure the butter is cold when making this "

Method

To make the pasrty case, sieve the flour, salt and icing sugar into a large bowl. Rub in the cold diced butter until it forms breadcrumbs. Whisk together the eggs and vanilla seeds and pass through a fine sieve. Make a well in the flour mix then add the eggs. Mix together, then knead on a clean surface until the pastry comes together, cover and leave to set in the fridge for at least a couple of hours.

Blind bake the case in the oven until cooked (180°C with baking beans on baking paper for about 15-20 mins). Remove the beans and finish baking for another 15-20 mins until golden brown.

For the filling, mix the sugar and milk together in an electric mixer on a medium speed until fully dissolved and the mix is light and fluffy (approx 5-8 mins).

Pour into the tart shell all the way to the top, cook in a pre-heated oven at 165°C (fan oven) for 10 minss. When cooked allow to cool on a wire rack.

For the lemon cream, whip the cream with zest and juice of the lemon until smooth and soft peak should form.

Will Devlin
The Small Holding

Holding

At The Small Holding our food philosophy is simple. Work with nature and produce. Grow the tastiest food with as little interference and use as much as we can from the woods and hedgerows. Changing our menus every few weeks depending on what's available makes it really exciting and keeps things changing all the time "

Will Devlin - Small Holding

PIGEON AND PRESERVES
A mix of sweet, crunch and acidity

Wood pigeon are shot locally to us all year round and are an amazing source of protein. With a delicate game flavour and super lean meat. We find that pigeon are best around September. To garnish as a wild feast use all of your pickles and preserves from the cupboard

Ingredients

Pigeon
1 x whole wild wood pigeon
100g smoked pork belly
1 small onion
Sprig of thyme
Sprig of rosemary
1 beaten egg
1 clove of garlic
150g yeast flakes
100g of bread crumbs
1 handful of dry oak bark and leaves from the woods
50g salt
50g sugar
1 teaspoon of black pepper
1 tablespoon pine needles
Wild leaf (we used chickweed, but anything with a peppery kick)

Preserves
We use our preserves that we have been storing in our larder over the past few months. We use all sorts. pickled beetroot, elderberry capers, fermented blueberries, wild nettle pesto, salted green strawberries, dried seeds and nuts.

You can use anything you have so long as it packs a punch.

> *Make sure you check the bird for any shots. This will be pretty hard to eat and not very delicious. But at least it means that is didn't just fall out of the sky*

Method

Using a food processor, blend together salt, sugar and pine needles to make a cure. Remove the breast from the pigeon. Cover pigeon breasts in the salt and sugar and leave the breasts to cure for 20 mins.

Bone out the pigeon legs, remove all skin and sinew. Mince the meat finely with a knife. Then mince together the garlic, thyme, rosemary, onion & pork belly. Then mix all ingredients with the minced pigeon legs. Add a generous pinch of salt and touch of black pepper.

Roll into balls and refrigerate until later.

Once the breasts are cured, wash off any excess salt and sugar and pat dry with kitchen towel.

Set up your smoker (this can be as basic as a tray with a resting rack and some tin foil). Add your oak and leaves, and when they are smoking well, add the breasts and smoke for 6 mins. When done, remove and rest.

Now to coat the leg in the dry yeast and breadcrumbs. Using a fork dip the balls in the egg, then drain as much egg off as possible. Roll in the bread and yeast mix until covered. Once coated we use a beech twig to fry our pigeon leg. The beech is such a fantastic tree and has lots of edible and medicinal properties, plus we have one on the farm. Sterilise your twig in boiling water for a few mins. Beech is perfectly safe, its just to make sure it's clean.
Skewer your pigeon leg ball with the beech twig and you are ready to plate.
Set the oven to 170°C and warm a pan of neutral oil (soy/vegetable) to 180°C

To assemble the dish just organise your preserves as you wish to on the plate. Crisp up the pigeon leg in the oil, warm the pigeon breast in the oven for 3-4 mins. Add breast and leg to the plate and serve. We use some leaves and twigs from the woods to serve in the restaurant.

BRAISED LAMB SHOULDER

Kent lamb shoulder, lamb broth and a milk stout rarebit

This dish is a proper winter warmer. A great way to warm up after a day out on the farm or walking in the woods. Beautiful Kent lamb broth with the ultimate cheese on toast! What more could you want?

Ingredients

Lamb

1 Kent lamb shoulder
1 bunch rosemary
1 bunch thyme
2 bulbs garlic
8 peppercorns
3ltr lamb stock
30g Maldon sea salt
100ml rapeseed oil
750ml red wine (Lee uses Tempranillo)

Lamb broth

400g lamb neck fillet, cut into small pieces
3kg lamb rib bones
1 large onion finely chopped
2 cloves garlic crushed
½ bunch thyme
½ bunch rosemary
80g pearl barley
4 ltr lamb stock

Milk stout rarebit

250g flour
50g butter
200g lamb fat
2 pints milk stout
2 pints milk
1 bay leaf
3 sprig thyme
3 cloves of garlic
1 shallot
2 peppercorns
2 cloves
1 tablespoon Dijon mustard
2 slugs of tabasco
2 slugs Worcestershire sauce
800g grated cheddar
4 egg yolks

> *You can use the bones from the cooked lamb shoulder again for another broth. And any left over lamb shoulder is amazing in a Shepherd's pie*

Method

Set the oven to 130°C. Season lamb shoulder with Maldon salt. Sear off the lamb shoulder in oil until golden brown and remove from the pan.
Cut the garlic bulbs in half and roast all the herbs and spices in the same pan you cooked the lamb in. Just to start the cooking add red wine to reduce slightly. Then add all the wine, herbs, and lamb stock into a large over tray with the lamb shoulder and braise in the oven for six hours at 130C. When cooked let cool and shred all meat off the bone and reserve for plating.

Roast off all ingredients together in a large thick bottom pan until coloured off and well roasted. Add the lamb stock and cook for 30 mins. Bring to the boil and reduce by half. Add pearl barley and cook for a further 20mins.

Ready to serve.

Make a roux with the lamb fat, butter and flour and cook out for five mins. Add bay leaf, thyme, garlic, shallot, peppercorns and cloves to the milk and bring to the boil. Slowly add the milk to the roux whilst stiring. Add grated cheese, mustard, tabasco and Worcestershire sauce and stir until the cheese is melted. Beat in the egg yolks and cool with a cartouche.

To serve, cut a chunky slice of bread and toast one side under the grill. Add the lamb shoulder mix to the top, before adding the lamb fat rarebit. Pop back under the grill until the rarebit starts to bubble.

Warm the broth up and put in a bowl or mug.

Settle down by the fire and warm yourself up!

Lee Edney
The Swan at West Malling

The Swan

I've always been a strong advocate of using fresh, local produce. Not only are you guaranteed a high-quality product but you're also supporting local businesses; businesses from your own community. One of our main suppliers is Spadework, a charity based just a couple of miles away, where adults with learning difficulties are given the opportunity to develop life skills through horticulture. They grow their own fruit and vegetables, which they then personally deliver to our kitchen. You become invested in their passion and that's reflected in their produce, as well as in the dishes we are able to create as a result.

Lee Edney - The Swan at West Malling

ROASTED CAULIFLOWER
Red lentil dhal, glazed shallot and mint yoghurt, with a raisin and pine nut dressing

A hearty vegetarian dish with a Indian influence. The roast cauliflower brings a meaty element to the dish with the spiced dhall. It's rounded off with a fresh mint yogurt and textured pine nut and raisin dressing

Ingredients

1 cauliflower,
1 thick slice and 1 large floret
Picked coriander

Dressing
5g pine nuts
5g golden raisins
5g raisins

Red lentil dhal
½ onion, finely chopped
1 garlic clove, finely chopped
2g ginger, grated
½ red chilli, finely chopped
¼ tablespoon turmeric
¼ tablespoon ground cumin
¼ tablespoon ground coriander
¼ tablespoons curry powder
¼ tablespoon garam masala
200g red lentils

Cauliflower pureé
½ cauliflower
50g unsalted butter
350ml milk - blue top
100g double cream

Mint yoghurt
10g mint yogurt
5 mint leaves, finely chopped

Roasted shallot
1 banana shallot, cut in half (keep skin on)
125g unsalted butter
Thyme 5 sprigs
2 garlic cloves

> *The mint yoghurt adds creaminess to the dish. Keep the cauliflower chunky as it is a replacement for meat*

Method

For the cauliflower slice and floret then poach in salted boiling water for 2-3 mins to soften the core of the cauliflower slice. Add 50g of butter to a heavy pan, place the cauliflower and floret in the pan and cook until golden.

For the red lentil dhal, sweat the red chilli, onion and garlic in a little olive oil, add all the spices and cook out for 1 min. Add lentils.

Cover with vegetable stock and gently cook down until the lentils are soft. Take off the heat and add 50g diced cold butter and stir into the lentil mix. Season with salt and a squeeze of lemon

For the califlower pureé, cut the cauliflower into small florets and slice the stalk thinly. Add to the cream, milk and butter and cook until the cauliflower is soft. Remove the cauliflower and blend using the poaching liquid to form a very smooth, silky pureé. Season with salt.

For the roasted shallot, melt the butter and garlic in a heavy pan, cut the shallot in half and place flesh side down in the pan. Add the thyme and gently roast. Once the shallot is golden brown and soft to touch remove from the pan and take off the outer skin.

For the pine nut and raisin dressing, lightly toast the pine nuts in the oven or grill until golden. Mix with both kinds of raisins. Add 2 tbsp of olive oil to bind together.

CHART FARM VENISON

Braised Puy lentils, braised red cabbage, cavolo nero & blackberry

This dish is simply a great pairing of robust and seasonal ingredients. The strong game flavour of the venison, which is sourced from Chart Farm in Sevenoaks, Kent, is complimented by the nutty, earthy taste of the lentils, with a shot of sweetness from the red cabbage and blackberries. It's a contemporary take on a classic combination

Ingredients

160g venison haunch
3 fresh blackberries
50g Cavolo Nero

Braised lentils

200g of Puy lentils, soaked for 30 mins before using and then drained
10g of carrots, peeled and diced
10g of celery, peeled and diced
1 shallot, diced
6g of thyme
1 bay leaf
3 juniper berries - crushed
2 garlic cloves, peeled
1 pinch of salt

Braised red cabbage

150g red cabbage, thinly sliced with the core removed
65ml red wine
50ml red wine vinegar
20g raisins
50g sugar
¼ Bramley apple, grated
10g honey

Lentils give a good earthy base to the dish. The lentils go well with the braised red cabbage, which we cook down like a chutney to give a beautiful sweet contrast

Method

For the venison, heat the olive oil in a pan and when hot sear the venison all over. Place in a pre-heated oven (190°C) for 4 mins then remove, baste with butter and allow to rest.

For the braised lentils, soak the lentils in cold water overnight then drain. Sweat off the celery, carrot and shallot in a little olive oil and add the juniper, garlic, bay leaf and thyme. Next add the lentils and cover with chicken or vegetable stock and cook gently until the lentils are slightly soft.

For the braised red cabbage, marinade all the ingredients for 24 hours. Gently cook on the stove until the cabbage is nice and soft. Once the cabbage is cooked, pass and reduce the remaining marinade (thicken with a little cornflour if necessary). Once thickened, mix back through the cabbage, this should coat and hold the red cabbage, with a glossy shine.

To plate, carve through the grain of the meat and place on top of the lentils. Garnish with fresh blackberries.

Patrick Hill
Head Chef at Thackeray's

Thackeray's

"As they say 'it's lonely at the top', so being head chef can be difficult as you no longer have someone above you to learn from. You need to do a lot more research to stay abreast of new cuts of meats and cooking methods, for example. New ways of cutting meat, such as rump steak, are always being championed. It's then a matter of applying your own identity to this new found knowledge to create something original, instead of just copying someone else. There is no point in merely replicating; you must try to continually improve.

A humble chicken can be very underrated. While a mediocre steak can still satisfy, chicken needs to be brined and cooked to perfection. However achieving crispy skin and succulent, tasty meat is actually quite hard to do. I love using garlic and lots of herbs in my cooking, which can really enhance the ingredients to bring out the cooked flavours.

Our fish comes from the markets for continuity, but we also buy from Hastings and Dungeness. We buy locally as much as possible depending on the season. It doesn't have to be all about luxury fish like sea bass and turbot. You can still find stunning quality with less expensive fish, such as mackerel and sea bream. Similarly Kent game is simply amazing and just as good as anywhere.

When it comes to local produce everyone champions their own favourites. I was lucky to be born and bred in Kent I still love what it has to offer here."

Patrick Hill - Thackeray's

MILK AND HONEY

Roast figs, milk sorbet, raw matfield honey, pistachios and dill

I wanted to champion the amazing honey we have on our doorstep so this dish was centred all around it. It's used throughout the recipe and finished with a generous drizzle at the table. This dish didn't need too much thought as the honey did the hard work for me! Thanks Liz (Home Grown Honey, Matfield)

Ingredients

Roasted figs
5 figs
50g butter
20ml Matfield honey

Milk sorbet
750ml milk
375g double cream
150g caster sugar
70g milk powder (dried milk)
50g glucose
20g dextrose

Dill oil
4 bunches fresh dill
300ml rapeseed oil
300ml vegetable oil

Dill sponge
8 eggs
30g caster sugar
90g Panko breadcrumbs
210g ground almonds
2tsp baking powder
400ml dill oil

Candied pistachio
100g sugar
Water to wet sand consistency
100g shelled pistachios

Honeycomb
160g caster sugar
2tsp glucose
20g Matfield honey
40ml water
20g bicarbonate of soda

Be creative and have fun. When plating dishes don't be too rigid; not every fig and pistachio will be the same size so just display them to their best

Method

First prepare the roasted figs. Place the butter in a pan and heat until foaming, add the figs (cut into sixths) and sear on each cut side, add the honey at the last 20 seconds and then pour all contents onto a tray and set aside.

For the milk sorbet, bring all the ingredients to the boil, chill over a bowl of ice and then churn in an ice cream machine according to the manufacturer's instructions.

For the dill oil, put the dill and the oils into a liquidiser and blitz on full for 5 mins. Hang all the contents in damp muslin cloth – what drips out is your dill oil (you'll need 400ml).

Now for the dill sponge. Pre-heat the oven to 170°C and prepare a 30x15x3cm tin by lining it with parchment paper. Create a sabayon with the eggs and sugar by whisking the egg yolks and the sugar together in a bowl over a bain-marie until a custard-like consistency. Fold in the dry ingredients followed by the oil, pour into the prepared tin and bake in the pre-heated oven for roughly 35-40 mins.

To make the candied pistachio, place the sugar in a pan, add a small amount of water until the sugar goes to a wet sand consistency. Boil until the bubbles in the mix get smaller, remove from the heat, add the pistachios and stir until the sugar and water candies around the nuts. Set aside until ready to serve.

Meanwhile make the honeycomb. Line a baking tray with parchment. In a saucepan heat the sugar, glucose, water and honey until it reaches 160°C then whisk in the bicarbonate of soda and pour the mix straight onto the parchment and leave to cool. Store in the freezer.

To assemble the dessert, be creative and have fun, when plating dishes they need to be fluid and not rigid, not every fig and pistatio will be the same size so just see what works well in different places.

Serve with a drizzle of Matfield honey.

SALT AND PEPPER SQUID

Squid, octopus, black olive tapenade and pickled shallot rings

I wanted to think outside the box a little with some more unusual flavours/ingredients, which are now growing in popularity. In particular octopus and yeast. Octopus is an excellent ingredient and very versatile which can carry many flavours. This dish was on the menu around autumn/winter so I went with the red wine braised addition, to add more depth and body. With the yeast element in the puree, this adds a nice 'zing' and freshness to the dish

Ingredients

Squid
8 baby squid
200g flour
Salt and pepper
100ml milk

Octopus
1 washed octopus
1 bottle of Biddenden Gribble Bridge Dornfelder
¼ bunch thyme
2 bay
3 cloves
1 star anise
3 cloves garlic
100g sugar

Black olive tapenade
500g pitted black olives
100g confit shallots
6 sprigs tarragon
4 sprigs thyme
Seasoning

Yeasted cauliflower
1 cauliflower
50g yeast extract
400ml chicken stock
400ml milk
Seasoning
2 shallots
1 clove garlic
2 sprigs thyme

Pickled shallot rings
4 long shallots
100ml white wine
100ml white wine vinegar
100g sugar
1 star anise
1 bay leaf

To serve
Cauliflower florets
Fennel pollen
Grapefruit segments

> *Assemble all the elements on the plate and have fun! There's no right or wrong way to plate; just be fluid and organic*

Method

First prepare the octopus by washing it from any grit or sea slim under a cold running tap.

Take the wine, sugar and all the aromats and reduce slowly until they form a syrup and cool down.

Place the octopus whole into a vacuum pac bag along with the red wine reduction and vacuum. If you don't have a vac pac then a sandwich bag will do just fine and leave to marinate in the fridge overnight.

To cook, if you have one, set your water bath to 78°C and cook for 5 hours. If you don't have a water bath, put the octopus into an oven proof dish with a lid, add 200ml of water and braise at 150°C for roughly 2 hours, checking when it is tender. Leave to cool in the liquid.

For the cauliflower puree, slice the shallot and chop the garlic and sweat in a pan with no colour, add the thyme and sliced cauliflower and sweat for a further 5 mins. Add the stock, milk and seasoning and simmer for 30 mins until the cauliflower is tender. Blitz cauliflower in a liquidiser adding the liquid slowly until smooth.

For the tapenade, put olives, herbs and shallots into the food processor and pulse until at the right consistency.

For the pickled shallots, slice the shallots into rings, boil the wine, vinegar and sugar with the aromats and pour over the shallots, this can be done months in advance and stored in a jar for better flavour.

For the squid, prep the tubes by slicing them in half and scoring into a diagonal pattern and store in the milk until time to serve.

Now everything is ready it's a case of getting it hot and making to look pretty. So cut the eight tentacles from the octopus and warm them in the liquor.

Remove your squid from the milk and add to the flour and seasoning. Remove and deep fry at 180°C until golden brown.

Plate.

Megs Buchanan
The 26 Restaurant

"As a chef I'm inspired by the places I've travelled to. My travel experiences are a massive part of who I am as a person and as a chef. It's an opportunity to tell a story from a place I've been or a moment I've had. Its broadened my thoughts on food and my ideas on how to do things. Living in Kent is a new opportunity to discover another region and what it has to offer. I don't feel there's a need to over complicate an ingredient or a dish, simply let the produce speak for itself, while harmonising flavours to create balance."

Megs Buchanan - The 26 Restaurant

SEA BREAM
Jerusalem Artichoke

It's winter; it's cold, and sitting by the fire in the restaurant I want something warm and comforting. I love bisque, which is why I wanted to have this dish on the menu for our cold English winter. I prefer cooking fish the old-fashioned way in a pan, basted with butter, with the wintery artichoke adding an earthy flavour. From a county surrounded by water why not use the local produce to marry it all together

Ingredients

4 fillets of sea bream

Lobster bisque
4 lobster heads
4 cloves garlic, sliced
2 sticks celery, roughly chopped
2 carrot, roughly chopped
1 medium onion, diced
1 heaped spoon tomato paste
1 cup brandy
1 cup white wine
3 star anise
5 cardamom pods
3lts fish stock
1 cup cream

Jerusalem artichoke
500g Jerusalem artichoke, peeled
5 springs thyme
Olive oil

Aioli
50g Confit garlic
200g mayonnaise

Jerusalem artichoke crisps
2 Jerusalem artichokes
Vegetable oil

Fennel cress

If you don't want to make the bisque then feel free to buy one (Waitrose I believe sell them) and add some cream

Method

For the lobster bisque, heat a large pot with a little oil, add garlic, celery, onion, carrot and spices, cook until lightly coloured and aromatic. Add lobster and cook for several mins. Add tomato paste and cook it out.

Deglaze the pot with the brandy and wine then reduce. Add the fish stock, bring to the boil, turn down to a simmer and cook for 20 mins. Strain the bisque through a sieve pushing down on the shells with a ladle till dry. Add the cream to the bisque and reduce by half and season.

For the Jerusalem artichoke, put all ingredients in a medium pot with a few pinches of salt and boil till the artichokes are soft. Strain and crush. When ready, heat with a small knob of butter.

To make the aioli, blend the garlic until smooth and mix through mayonnaise.

Jerusalem Artichoke Crisps. Heat the oil in a deep fryer to 150°C and thinly slice the artichoke on a mandolin. Fry in batches until crispy.

Drain on a J-cloth and season lightly with salt.

To plate, heat a large pan with oil then season the fish on both sides.
When the pan is lightly smoking add the fish, skin side down, pushing the fish down so it doesn't curl up.

Cook the fish so the flesh is cooked ¾ of the way up, turn the fish over, add a table spoon full of butter and baste the fish. Place on a J-cloth and rest for a few mins.

Meanwhile heat the Jerusalem artichoke's and bisque.

Spoon even amounts of artichoke into bowls and pour the bisque around the artichoke Once the fish is rested place on top of the artichoke with a spoon of aioli and the artichoke chips.

Garnish with fennel cress.

ARTICHOKE PARFAIT

Roast figs, milk sorbet, raw Matfield honey, pistachios and dill

The parfait dish was developed after reflecting on root vegetable desserts, such as carrot cake and pumpkin pie. Then it was choosing a form, either cake or cream based, thinking about how best to highlight the flavour as it become a parfait. Adding garnishes to the dish required thinking about what went with the artichoke when it's used in a savoury role, which is where the coffee came in. Adding the chestnut was a textural need that matched well with the season and flavour of the artichoke, while the pear added a sweeter, dessert element, as well as including produce from Kent

Ingredients

Parfait
300g Jerusalem artichoke puree
150g sugar
120g egg yolk
750ml water
150ml cream, whipped to soft peaks

Coffee crumb
112g plain flour
60g cornflour
60g light brown sugar
2 tbs fresh ground coffee
112g butter

Pear pureé
4 pears
100g sugar

Fresh ground coffee

2 chestnuts, roasted

Fold this together gently to keep the air in otherwise it will be too hard and dense

Method

To make the parfait, bring the sugar and water to 120°C.
Meanwhile whisk the yolks until doubled, pour in the hot sugar mix and whisk until cold. Once cold, fold through the pear puree then the whipped cream and freeze in a lined terrine mould.

For the coffee crumb, mix the flours and butter to a crumb and add the sugar and coffee. Crumb the mixture onto a lined baking tray and cook at 160°C for 20 mins, stirring at 5 minute intervals and leave to cool.

Pear pureé. Peel and roughly chop the pears, removing the core. Cook the pears with the sugar until translucent and blend until smooth.

To Plate, slice a 2cm thick piece of parfait and arrange on a plate. Spoon a spoonful full of coffee crumb over the parfait and dot 4 to 5 spots of pear pureé around and on the parfait. Slice a few pieces of pear thinly and arrange on the dish, then crumble the chestnut over the top.

Very lightly sprinkle some fresh coffee over the whole dessert.

Three Mariners

Ryan Tasker
Three Mariners

"

Cooking is not only about the recipe, but looking for the best ingredients at the right time of the year, respecting them when you cook and serving them simply, in context and for everybody.

The Three Mariners is commitment to sustainability, traceability and the environment works hand in hand with our teams philosophy of supporting local, British producers and working with ethical suppliers, who are experts in their fields.

Aiming for food excellence, introducing our customers to some of the finest artisan producers in Kent and the bountiful countryside beyond.

I would describe my cooking as 'free flowing and natural, concentrating on delivering the best flavour possible'. Seasonal cooking really excites me, as does using the freshest possible ingredients I can get my hands on.

"

Ryan Tasker - Three Mariners

FILLET STEAK
Stockpot carrots, smoked oxtail, parmentier potatoes

From the fresh-from-the fields vegetables to the choicest cuts from our local butcher, we can trace back to its roots every morsel of top-quality food cooked to perfection. So when you sit down to enjoy one of our succulent, juicy fillet's, cooked just the way you like it, served with fresh-from-the soil mushrooms, tomatoes, and potatoes, you can relax in the knowledge that we are all doing our bit to preserve the planet's dwindling resources.

Ingredients

Steak
4oz fillet steak (1 per person)
Salt & pepper

Oxtail and stockpot carrot
1 oxtail cut into two inch pieces
1 onion, peeled and roughly cut
½ celery stick, rough cut
1 bulb of garlic, cut in half
4 large carrots, peeled, topped and tailed (keep whole)
1 bottle of red wine
2 litres of chicken stock
Bay leaf
Sprig of thyme
Salt and pepper

Parmentier potatoes
4 large peeled potatoes
Thyme
2 cloves of garlic
Salt and pepper

As the steak is a small cut (4oz) the pan should be searing hot to caramelise the steak quickly, the colour is where the majority of the flavour is. This process should only take a few mins to achieve medium rare

Method

Place the oxtail in a smoker on a low heat of 55°C and smoke for 2 hours.
Then in a hot pan sear the oxtail to get a good colour on it. Place it in a deep roasting tray.

Sear the vegetables in the same hot pan as the oxtail then add to the roasting tray. Cover with stock, wine and herbs. Then braise in the oven for 4 hours until the meat is failing off the bone.

Drain off the oxtail, keeping the liquor to reduce down for the sauce. Pick the meat off the bone and also pick out the carrots and set aside.

In this dish I have added fine diced carrot and shallot to the oxtail, also a little of the reduced liquor, wrapped 100g portions in caul fat and baked in the oven for 8 mins before serving.

Now the stockpot carrot. With the carrot removed from the oxtail, cut to desired size. Reheat in a little stock, season and serve.

Place the steaks in a hot frying pan and season. Flash fry until your desired degree ie, medium rare etc.

CONFIT BELLY OF PORK
Rosemary mash

Pork belly, like bacon, starts out from the underside or the belly of the pig. Consider it far tastier and superior to cured and smoked bacon. Pork belly has juicy fat layers wrapped around the meat. There isn't much meat, but once cooked it becomes tender, similar in texture to a pork loin. And that fat is melt-in-your-mouth. For optimum crackling, cook for longer at the higher temperature before reducing

Ingredients

Pork belly

Roast parsnips
4 parsnips
150g butter
1 tbsp honey

Rosemary mash
4 potatoes
100ml cream
100g butter
1 tsp chopped rosemary

Crackling
Pork skin
50g Maldon sea salt
10g fennel seeds

Low and slow....
This is the ethos for the pork belly, the timing has a two hour window due to not all being the same. Some are thick, thin, shorter and some long, you'll know when its done when you gently push a utensil through the meat

Method

Pork belly. Trim the pork belly of excess fat. Score the skin and salt for at least three hours. Wash and dry the pork belly. Place in large roasting tin, add herbs & garlic and lightly season. Cover with duck fat then tin foil & place in the oven at a low heat (110°C) and cook for 6 to 8 hours until tender. Remove from oven and drain off fat.

Place another tray on top of the pork, then add a light weight on top of the tray. Leave to press in the fridge for a few hours.

Pork belly. Once taken from the fridge, remove skin and keep. Then cut to desired size. I cut to 1.5 inch cubes as when this size they only take about 10 mins to reheat. To reheat, heat pan on moderate heat, add pork then add butter. The butter should be a golden foam. Keep turning the pork until each side is crispy.

Roast parsnips. Peel & cut parsnips to desired size. Keep trimmings (not peelings), for pureé later. Similar procedure as the pork belly, put in a pan with foaming butter except at the end, when cooked, glaze with honey.

Rosemary mash. Peel and cut the potatoes. Boil in water for 25 mins until soft. Drain and mash. Meanwhile, infuse the cream with the chopped rosemary on a low heat, add this to the potato. Cube the butter and add piece by piece. Season to taste.

Crackling. Take the skin from the belly and scrape off the excess fat underneath. Cut into long thin strips, lay flat on a baking tray lined with parchment paper. Sprinkle with salt and fennel seeds. Cover with parchment paper and another baking tray then bake for 25 mins at 180°C.

Scott Gross
Verdigris

"I have been a chef for over 20 years working with some of the best chefs in the country; starting with Gary Rhodes, Andrew Clarke, Anton Edlemann and Robert Spencer, cooking classic British, French and other European style food. Growing up in The Garden of England, I spent much of my time out in the countryside apple picking, lamping and foraging for wild food. My appreciation and love of Mother Nature is evident in my food at Verdigris, which showcases my passion for using only the freshest seasonal and locally sourced ingredients.

When I cook I have two rules: You're only as good as the ingredients you choose to cook and to

SMOKED HADDOCK AND LEEK SOUP
Slow cooked egg

We're showcasing humble, relatively inexpensive everyday ingredients

Ingredients

50g salted butter
500g natural smoked haddock with the skin on
5 baby leeks
15g chives
10g thyme
6 eggs: Clarence Court Old Cotswold Legbar free range blue eggs
(1 egg per serving)
500ml double cream
200ml full fat milk
330ml bottle of Jakes Cider
1 large banana shallot
2 cloves of garlic
1 bay leaf
Kentish rapeseed oil
Cracked black pepper

" Buy natural smoked haddock. Find a good local dry cider. For the perfect poached eggs boil lots of water in a big pan then add the vinegar before whisking the water to create a vortex to drop the eggs into. Don't use refrigerated eggs but ones that have been left out at room temperature "

Method

Skin the haddock.
Peel and slice the shallots and garlic. In a large saucepan add 50g of butter.
Warm the butter over medium heat and add a splash of rapeseed oil, the shallots, garlic, thyme, bay leaf and haddock skin. Sweat down the ingredients in the butter for $2\frac{1}{2}$ mins until the shallots are translucent.

Add 200ml of the Kentish Jakes Cider....(drink the rest!) Reduce the cider down until approx 50ml is left in the pan. Add the double cream and add the milk.

Slowly bring to the boil. Take straight off the heat and let it cool down until cold. Now that the flavours have infused pass the sauce through a fine sieve three times.

Take the passed sauce, add the haddock to the sauce and gently poach for 4-6 mins until the fish starts to flake.

Finely slice the baby leeks and snip the chives. Add to the soup and stir.

Bring a pan of water to the boil, add a splash of white wine vinegar and poach the eggs for $2\frac{1}{2}$ mins.

To serve, place a poached egg in the bottom of each bowl. Place the saucepan of haddock soup next to the egg and spoon over the egg.

Enjoy with crusty bread.

BEETROOT 'STONE' TRUFFLES
Chocolate soil

We are highlighting the versatility of the wonderful beetroot, making a fun dessert which will bring a smile to peoples faces

Ingredients

Ganache
350ml beetroot juice
50ml double cream
2g rosemary
200g white chocolate

Chocolate soil
80g caster sugar
80g ground almonds
60g plain flour
40g cocoa powder
65g salted butter

White chocolate mousse
225g Philadelphia soft cheese
75g caster sugar
125g crème fraîche
225g double cream
150g white chocolate

Frozen yoghurt
1 small pot of Greek yoghurt
2 tablespoons of maple syrup

To serve
In the restaurant we do a Roche of white chocolate mousse on a small plate. Using a fine grater we then grate the frozen yogurt over the top of the mousse.
To the side we add a beetroot truffle. We then spoon the chocolate soil over the top of the beetroot truffle.

For the perfect Roche place your large dessert spoon into boiling water for 30 seconds. Make the truffles and chocolate soil the day before you need them

Method

For the 'stone' beetroot truffles, add the beetroot juice and rosemary to a pan. Reduce the beetroot juice down to 100ml with the rosemary. Bring the double cream to the boil and reduce by half. Pour the beetroot juice into the double cream. Whisk to emulsify.
In a bowl add 150g of white chocolate. Bring the beetroot and double cream back to the boil. When it has reached boiling point add to the white chocolate. Whisk until you have a beautiful smooth ganache. Pour the ganache out of the saucepan and onto a baking tray. Put into the fridge to set overnight.

For the frozen yoghurt, mix the maple syrup through the Greek yogurt. Put into a bowl, cover and place in the freezer overnight.

To make the mousse, in a baine-marie gently melt the white chocolate. In a different bowl take the Philadelphia cream cheese, sugar, crème fraîche, double cream and whisk together until it resembles a light shaving foam consistency; this is your mousse. Then take one tablespoon of the mousse and mix it through the melted chocolate. Once that tablespoon has been thoroughly mixed into the melted chocolate add another tablespoon of mousse, mix and repeat until all of the mousse has been incorporated into the white chocolate. Pour into a container and place in the fridge.

For the chocolate soil, mix the dry ingredients together. Melt the butter in a pan. Pour the melted butter over the top of the dry ingredients and mix through. Lay out the mixed ingredients onto a flat tray lined with baking paper. Bake at 160°C for half and hour, ensuring you move the mixture around the tray every 10 mins to stop it from burning. Allow to cool then transfer to an airtight container.

Ball up the beetroot ganache by taking a teaspoon and dragging it backwards across the tray then rolling it in your hands until it resembles a round stone or truffle shape. Place onto a clean tray. Once you have done this with all of the ganache put the stone shaped balls back into the fridge for another hour.
Meanwhile with the remaining 50g of white chocolate, melt in a bain-marie. Remove the beetroot truffles from the fridge, place a toothpick into a beetroot truffle and dip into the melted white chocolate. Place back onto the tray. Remove the toothpick and repeat the process for each truffle. Leave the truffles on the tray until the chocolate has set, then refrigerate.

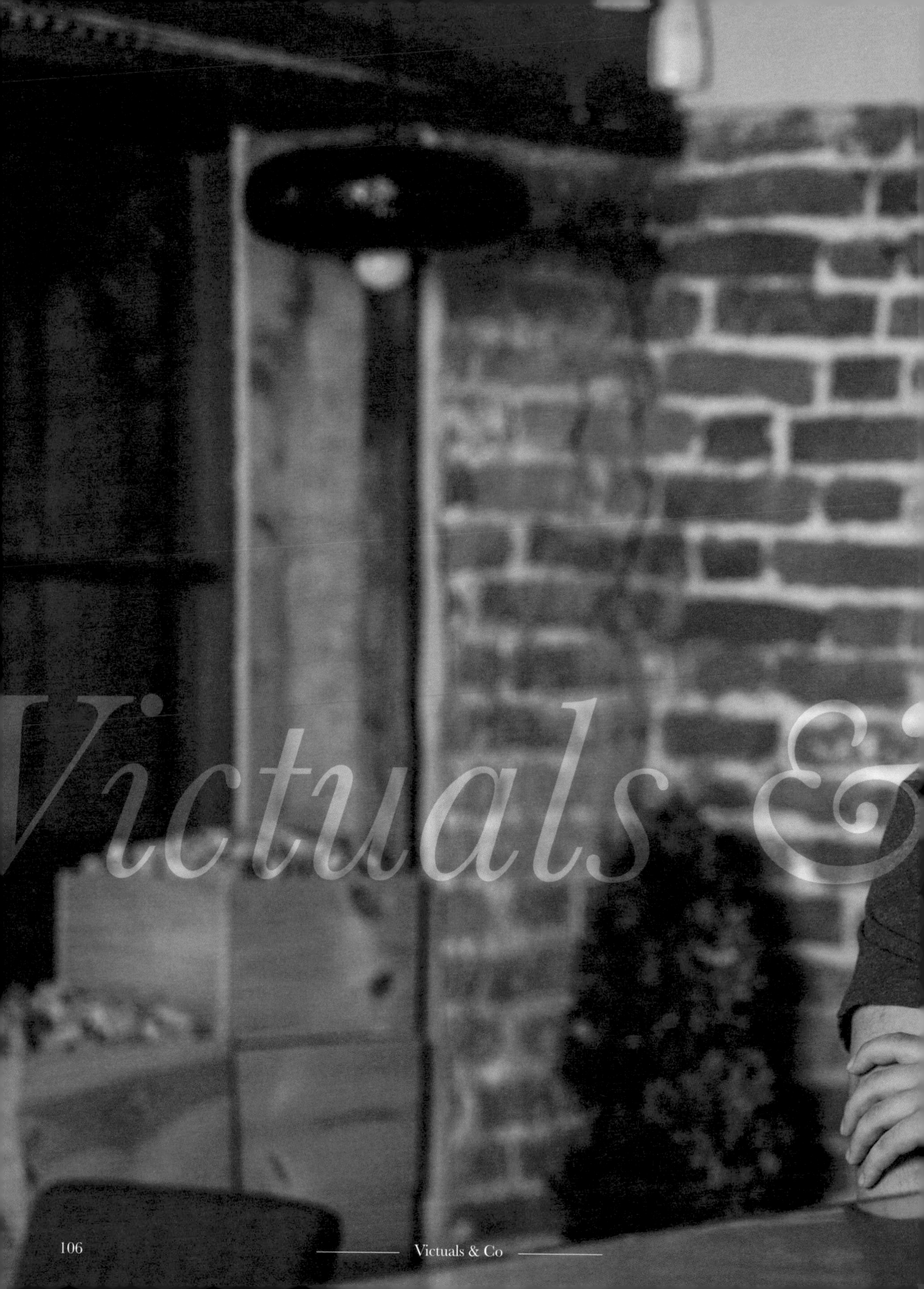
Victuals &

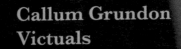

Callum Grundon
Victuals

I'm a young chef and I feel there is so much more to learn. Everyday there is a new lesson to be learnt. Experimenting as a team is something I really enjoy doing.
I have already travelled many times to south east Asia, as well as other countries. I've discovered that some of the most simple ingredients can sometimes produce the deepest flavours. I love the fusion of many different styles of cooking. I love cooking and always look forward to what I can make next.

Callum Grundon - Victuals & Co

MACKEREL
Two ways

Personally I think mackerel is a very underrated fish. With its intensity of flavour it can be used for so many recipes. I wanted to show two ways of using the fish; firstly with the pâté and mixing it with other ingredients and then using lemon zest to lift it. The mackerel fillet really speaks for itself, using the crispy onions for texture, while the apple cuts a natural sweetness through the salt. The fillet is finished with the peppery kick of radish.

Ingredients

Mackerel pâté
1 pack smoked mackerel (250g)
1 small cream cheese (180g)
½ lemon zest and juice
½ tablespoon chopped dill
Pinch crackedblack pepper
50ml double cream

Apple jelly
240ml organic apple juice
3 leaves geletine

Pickled shallot rings
1 whole shallot sliced
100ml white wine vinegar
50ml water
50g sugar
6 whole peppercorns
6 fennel seeds
6 whole coriander seeds
1 bay leaf

Grilled mackerel
Two fresh fillets mackerel (pin boned)
Pinch of salt

To garnish
2 small radish
Toasted bread crumbs
Crispy shallots
Sesame seeds

Getting a good char on the crispy mackerel skin adds a really delicious chargrill flavour to the dish

Method

De-skin the smoked mackerel, check for bones, flake the smoked mackerel into a bowl.
Zest ½ lemon and the juice into bowl. Add ½ tablespoon of chopped dill then add 180g of cream cheese. Mix and then whip 50ml of double cream into soft peaks in a separate bowl. Fold into cream cheese to make it light and add cracked black pepper to finish. Place into a piping bag for easier plating.

For the apple jelly, soak 3 geletine leaves in cold water for 5 mins and bring the apple juice to the boil. Add soft geletine leaves and whisk off the heat until dissolved. Pour into a shallow tray, to make a thin layer of jelly between ½ cm thick
Leave to cool for ½ hour in the fridge to set. It will need 1-2 hours depending upon your fridge tempreture.

Now for the pickled shallot rings. Peel the shallot, take off the top and bottom and thinly slice before placing in a container. In a pan, place the white wine vinegar, water, sugar, peppercorns, fennel seeds, coriander seeds and bay leaf. Bring to the boil, and pour over raw shallot rings and cling film immediately. Leave to cool and infuse for 2 hours.

To plate, cut each fillet of mackerel into three, so six pieces in total. Gently score the skin and salt. Grill for 3½ mins (or until cooked) Leave to rest for 1 min.

In the meantime, pipe on mackerel pate on one half of the plate. Top the pate with thinly sliced radish. Remove jelly from the container and cut into 1.5cm cubes and top with sprinkles of sesame seeds. Add five of these to plate next to the pate.

Take three shallot rings out of pickling liquor, pat dry and place opposite the pate. Top the grilled mackerel with bread crumbs and crispy shallots, then carefully place on top of the shallot rings.

BEETROOT TARTARE
Celeriac purée, smoked almond

This dish was created coming out of the autumn season, heading into winter. It's always tough around this time of year as there is so little produce to work with. Using the beetroot, I wanted to create a rich, full flavoured dish without meat. Roasting the beetroot brings out a sweet, earthy flavour and then mixing in acidity makes a beautifully rich umami flavour. The grated smoked almond and toasted breadcrumbs give the dish that extra texture and another layer of smokiness

Ingredients

4 raw beetroot
½ celeriac
50ml double cream
1 tablespoon mirin (sweet rice wine)
1 tablespoon white wine vinegar
1 tablespoon soy sauce
100ml port
6 eggs
Salt
Pepper
10g Smoked almond
10g Bread crumbs

Wear gloves when working with beetroot and to get skins off use a dry piece of kitchen towel to create the grip

Method

Pre heat oven 180°C, individually wrap each beetroot in baking foil with salt to season.

Cook for 1 hour and leave to cool for ½ hour. Peel off the skin (preferably with gloves on), and dice into roughly 1cm cubes. Leave in a bowl and place to one side.

Then make the celeriac purée by peeling and dicing ½ celeriac. Boil until soft (20-25 mins approx). Drain water and add to the blender with 50ml of cream. Blend until smooth and season to taste.

For the port reduction, reduce 100ml port until a syrup-like consistency.

Mix in the mirin, white wine vinegar, and soy sauce, shake almost like a cocktail to make a dressing.

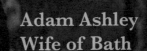

**Adam Ashley
Wife of Bath**

"Our philosophy on food is to always use the best locally sourced ingredients and we marry them with the best ingredients from Spain, such as picante chorizo, spicy morcilla and the amazing Iberian meats. This way we have high quality ingredients and support our local suppliers. A couple of our suppliers are: Fresher by Miles, who supply use with all our fresh fruit and vegetables and lots of Kentish produce and Chapmans, who supply us with our amazing fish most of it caught along the south coast. Both companies are Kent based and it's important we support local businesses. When suppliers take the time and care to produce great ingredients it gives you the passion to make the best you can from it."

Adam Ashley - Wife of Bath

IBERICO PORK
Wild mushrooms, cauliflower, morcilla, romesco

The idea behind this dish was to make the best we could of this amazing meat. It has so much flavour and can be matched with lots of different ingredients. The morcilla complements it well, as it has a spicy note to it, while the roasted wild mushrooms add more depth of flavour to the dish

Ingredients

Pork
500g Iberico pork piece
200g mixed wild mushrooms sliced
½ cauliflower
200g morcilla
50g butter
200ml vegetable stock
1 shallot finely diced
1 clove of garlic finely diced
1 egg beaten
40g plain flour
40g panko breadcrumbs

Romesco sauce
4 Piquillo peppers roasted skinned and deseeded
250g small vine tomatoes
15g blanched almonds
120ml olive oil
4 garlic cloves peeled
15g white sliced bread
½ tsp Knorr chilli paste
1 tbsp of sherry vinegar
½ tsp salt

> *Make the pork the star of the plate. Carve into thick slices and spread out on the plate. Then arrange the garnishes around it. You want to be able to see that amazing meat*

Method

Begin by making the Romesco sauce. Heat the oven to 180°C, put the tomatoes on a baking tray with the peppers. Drizzle with a tbsp of olive oil and season with sea salt and pepper. Wrap the garlic in foil and add to the tray and roast for 20 mins. When cool, pop the garlic out of the skin and leave to one side.
Toast the almonds until lightly browned. Heat the oil in a pan and fry the bread on both sides. Put the chilli paste, peppers, tomatoes, garlic, almonds, bread and vinegar into a blender and blend. Add 100ml of olive oil and blitz until smooth. Season with plenty of sea salt and black pepper.

Pre heat a fryer or a large saucepan to 180°C.
Next prep the Iberico pork. Begin by trimming any excess fat off the pork. Don't discard it as it can be used to fry the pork with later. Portion the pork into roughly 4 x 125g pieces. Once portioned place into the fridge till needed.

Next let's make the mushrooms, firstly place a large frying pan onto the heat. You want the pan quite hot so it will fry the mushrooms and get a good flavour. Once the pan is hot add a little oil and then the mushrooms. Allow to cook for 2-3 mins, stirring occasionally. Then add the chopped shallots and garlic and cook for a further 2-3 mins. Now add the butter followed by the vegetable stock. Allow these to cook for 10-15 mins.

While they are cooking prep the cauliflower into florets and blanch in boiling water for 4-5 mins and then refresh in iced cold water.

Next place the morcilla into a large mixing bowl and season with salt and pepper. Divide the mixture into 4 x 50g balls and then place into flour, egg and breadcrumbs.

Cook the pork by placing a large pan onto the heat. Add the saved pork trim, making sure the pan is hot. Add the seasoned pork and cook for 2 mins on each side to a golden caramelised colour. Add the blanched cauliflower to the same pan and then place onto a baking tray and cook for 2 mins. The pork needs to be around 65°C once it comes out of the oven before resting it for 5-10 mins. You want the pork to be pink in the middle, rest it till 45°C, you can always cook it for longer if you prefer.

To serve, slice the pieces of pork into three and arrange on the plate, next place the cauliflower on to the plate with a few spoonfuls of the romesco sauce. Then add the wild mushrooms with some of the sauce and the crispy morcilla ball.

RABBIT, CHORIZO, SAVOY CABBAGE, ROMESCO SAUCE

The thought process behind this dish actually came from Mark Sargeant a couple of years ago when we first opened and we have developed the dish from there. It has became a staple dish on our menu. Simplicity in presentation makes it stand out more; not overly complicated. The rabbit works so well with the spicy chorizo and we finish the rabbit with tarragon to add that nice aniseed flavour to the dish. We finish it with romesco sauce that compliments it well

Ingredients

4 cabbage leaves
1 chicken breast
½ bunch parsley, picked and finely chopped
½ bunch tarragon picked and finely chopped
50g chorizo diced
50g rabbit leg meat
50ml cream
Maldon sea salt

Romesco sauce

4 piquillo peppers roasted skinned and deseeded
250g small vine tomatoes
15g blanched almonds
120ml olive oil
4 garlic cloves peeled
15g white sliced bread
½ tsp Knorr chilli paste
1 tbsp of sherry vinegar
½ tsp salt

Serves 4

> *Don't over complicate the plate. The simplicity of this dish is what makes it stand out*

Method

Firstly cook the rabbit legs until tender and remove the meat from the bone. Make the chicken mousse by putting the chicken breast and salt together in a mixer and blend until smooth. Slowly add the cream and mix till smooth and pass through a sieve.

Sweat down the chorizo.

Into a mixing bowl put the rabbit leg, chorizo, parsley, tarragon, salt and pepper. Add the chicken mousse to bind. Blanch the cabbage leaf. Roll the mousse mixture into a 60g ball, and place in the middle of the cabbage leaf. Fold the cabbage leaf around the mix and roll into a ball. Cook for 10 mins till the chicken mousse is cooked.

Heat the oven to 180°C. Put the tomatoes on a baking tray with the peppers. Drizzle with a tbsp of olive oil and season with sea salt and pepper. Wrap the garlic in foil and add to the tray and roast for 20 mins. When cool, pop the garlic out of the skin and leave to one side.

Toast the almonds until lightly browned.

Heat the oil in a pan and fry the bread on both sides. Put the chilli paste, peppers, tomatoes, garlic, almonds, bread and vinegar into a blender and blend. Add 100ml of olive oil and blitz till smooth. Season with plenty of sea salt and black pepper.

To finish, spoon some of the Romesco sauce into the base of a large bowl, place the stuffed cabbage on top. Arrange eight in number flaked almonds around the cabbage and finish with chopped coriander.

Craig Edgell
Wyatt & Jones

Jones

"It's taken years to gradually achieve my goal of becoming a head chef. It may be my dishes which we create in the kitchen but it's the team behind me in which puts them on the plate. It feels like I have two families; home and work and I'm always dad! Sure we have ups and downs and it's hard graft, no doubt, but putting a new dish on the pass is a real achievement. We get to work with awesome suppliers from bakers to butchers, fruiterers to fishmongers. Our suppliers all have great knowledge, not just of local produce but I often find there's a whole library of knowledge. I am born and bred in Kent, so I see Kent as my canvas, where I can use the produce from what's on our doorstep.

My passion is fish, which has developed over the years. The sea is a constant unknown; you never know what your going to get. Seasons change and the ever changing weather affects the fishermen's catch. My favourite fish is mackerel, not only a beautiful fish but so robust too. Brined, pickled, smoked, roastd, pan fried. It can take them all but it must also be respected."

Craig Edgell - Wyatt & Jones

MACKEREL
Harissa sauce

Cook the mackerel in a hot, oiled pan skin side down until the skin is crisp. Turn over to the flesh side, remove from the heat and allow the residual heat in the pan to do the work. Mackerel has lots of fine bones so check and double check they're all removed. A customer finding a bone is not the end of the world but its best avoided

Ingredients

Mackerel
4 whole mackerel filleted and pinned boned
Vegetable oil

Harissa
20g dried chilli flakes
200g onions
1 tsp garlic purée
1 small tin chopped tomatoes
150g dark brown sugar
1 tbsp tomato paste
Salt
Vegetable oil

Celeriac, radish and apple
250g grated celeriac
4x diced radish
1x grated Granny Smith apple
pepper
salt
300g mayonnaise
1 tbsp lemon juice

Pickled shallots and Radish
2x banana shallots, sliced into rings
4x radish sliced
200ml white wine vinegar
200g caster sugar
(1x star anise, 1x cinnamon stick, 4x cloves)

Almond purée
100g almonds whole
1 tbsp garlic puree
350ml olive oil
150ml vegetable oil
1 tin of chick peas
2 tbsp chopped corriander
Salt
Pepper

Coriander cress for garnish

> *When cooking the fish flesh side down remove the pan from the heat. This lower heat allows the mackerel to rest at the same time*

Method

Harissa. In a sauce pan, fry the onion, garlic and dried chilli flakes until soft. Add the chopped tomatoes, tomato paste and sugar. Simmer until thick with a slight glaze. Allow to cool in fridge for 2-3 hours or overnight.

Celeriac remoulade. In a bowl, add the grated celeriac, radish and apple. With a spatula fold in the mayonnaise until coleslaw consistency. Add salt and pepper to taste, and lemon juice.

For the pickled shallots and radish, in a heavy bottomed pan, add the sugar, vinegar and aromats and bring to the boil. Once boiled and all sugar dissolved, take off the hear allow to cool slightly. Once cooled, pour over the shallots and radish in a bowl and set to the side.

Almond purée. Put the garlic, almonds, chickpeas the coriander into a food processer and blitz. Slowly add the mixed olive oil and vegetable oil. This will slowly create a emulsion and slowly thicken to a paste. Season to taste.

Mackerel. In a all-metal fish pan heat the pan to a medium heat with the oil. Place the mackerel skin side down when oil is hot cook for 2 mins then turn. Once turned, take a spoonful of harissa and spread across the skin.

Place the pan under a grill or pop in the oven to glaze the harissa, cook for a further 1 minute.

Once cooked, remove the fish from the pan and allow to rest in a warm area.

Serves 8

TRADITIONAL

Kent Rarebit
Serves 4

Ingredients:
100g grated Kentish Blue cheese
150g crème fraîche
A Kent Huffkin

2 free range Kent eggs
2 Kent eating apples

Method:
Whisk the egg yolks and crème fraîche together then mix in the grated cheese and some seasoning.

Slice your apples and very lightly soften then in a pan but make sure they hold there shape.

Lightly toast slices of Huffkin on both sides and place the apple slices on top. Spoon on the cheese mixture and place under a hot grill until the cheese mixture starts to bubble.

Canterbury Tart
Prepare or buy enough pastry to fill your tart tin

Ingredients:
4 free range eggs
200g caster sugar
2 organic lemons, rind and juice only, grated
100g melted Kent butter
2 large peeled Bramley apples
3 dessert apples, peeled and thinly sliced
25g demerara sugar

Method:
Pre-heat the oven to 200°C
For the filling beat the eggs, caster sugar, lemon rind and juice in a large mixing bowl and add the melted butter. Add grated Bramley apples to the bowl and mix well. Paste the mixture over over the pastry base evenly.

Place the dessert apple slices around the edge overlapping then sprinkle the demerara sugar over the top.

Place on a solid baking tray and bake for circa 45 mins until the apples are just browning and the centre is feeling solid.

KENT RECIPES

Creamy Cherry Almond and Choc Chip Ice

Instagram: Creamby the_smallseed

Ingredients:

1 cup raw cashews   300g Kent cherries (pitted)
155g coconut cream   160g medjool dates
1 teaspoon extract
30g cooked beetroot (optional for colour)
small handful of chopped dark chocolate

Method:

Rinse and drain the cashews. Add all ingredients except the choclate in a high-speed blender and blend until smooth and creamy. Place in a freezer safe dish and gently stir in the chocolate.

Place lid on and freeze overnight.
Take it out the freezer 10 mins before eating and sprinkle over the chocolate.

Kentish Cherry Batter Pudding

serves 6

Ingredients:

500g ripe dessert cherries   2 tablespoons dark rum
60g plain flour   pinch of salt
60g caster sugar   25g unsalted butter, melted
300ml milk   2 eggs, separated

Method:

Pour the batter over, so it comes nearly to the top (the deeper your dish, the less visible the cherries will be in the cooked pudding). Bake for 15 mins for small dishes, or 25-30 mins for one dish, till puffed and lightly set. Serve straight from the oven for maximum drama, with a generous sprinkle of rum and a thick dusting of icing sugar — it's particularly delicious with crème fraîche.

Pre-heat the oven to 190°C. Pour the rum over the stoned cherries. Mix the flour with the sugar and whisk in the milk and egg yolks to make the batter. Whisk the egg whites until stiff in a separate bowl and then fold in. Put a 25x20cm baking dish in the over to warm through and the add a knob of butter to coat the sides and base.

Place the cherries in the baking tray and pour over the batter and bake for around 25-30 mins.
Serve with your favourite vanilla ice cream.

JACK'S VEG

I first met Jack at a food fair in Canterbury in late 2018 and took to him immediately. He is at one with the ground with a huge passion for growing and sustainability. On visiting his mixed farming enterprise in the heart of Canterbury (started in 2012), I immediately thought how much my wife, Sarah, would like it. A field full of chickens roaming freely and producing trayfuls of egg; a large field full of carefully nurtured vegetables; mushrooms being cultivated in an old barn and trays of herbs growing in the winter sun. It really is the Good Life utopia but on a commercial scale.

Jack produces a large variety of fruit and veg. Meanwhile his mixed heritage breeds of poultry have been famed for their mixed coloured shells and firm golden yolks. Jack focuses on growing for nutrition and flavour with the aim to be certified Organic by the Soil Association. He is a firm believer in mixed farming systems, providing balance, fertility and order, whereas all too often artificial cultivation is the first 'go to' option. I believe it is important to support people like Jack, not only do you help the environment (less food miles), but you get better food to enjoy. I chatted with Jack the pleasures of home growing and asked him for a few tips that would benefit everyone :-

"If you love the idea of growing your own, it's really easy to have fresh greens all year from either a small pot on your kitchen windowsill to a few types of salad leaf grown on your allotment or garden. There are many types of lettuce that do well in cooler/cold climates and lower light conditions. Varieties like All Year Around, North Pole, Grenobloise and my favourite obviously- Jack Frost! Lettuce are light feeders meaning they don't need very fertile soil and do well in a shallow tray or plant pot on the window sill. Sow a few seeds every month or so and you can have lettuce all year around. Salads and herbs like coriander and mint also do well in a pot. Coriander does go to seed very quickly so it's a good idea to sow seed every 3 weeks or so to have a continual supply. It also doesn't mind the frost. Coriander can also keep some lettuce pests away if you grow them close together and you'll get less aphids that like to suck the sap of the lettuce.'

You can order a veg box direct to your door from the farm at jacksveg.co.uk.

JOBO BAKES
Strawberry shortbread cake

A fabulous cake for the summer, with beautiful shortbread bisucuit and strawberry Swiss meringue buttercream

Ingredients

Strawberry shortbread biscuit
150g unsalted butter
75g caster sugar
175g plain flour
50g cornflour
2 tbsp freeze dried strawberries
(optional)
¼ tsp salt

Strawberry filling, coulis & syrup
400g strawberries, plus a few extra
for decoration
120g sugar
Juice of half a lemon

Cake
Unsalted butter (roughly 300g)
Caster sugar (roughly 300g)
Self-raising flour (roughly 300g)
6 eggs (any size)
1.5 tsp baking powder
1.5 tsp vanilla extract
3 tsp whole milk (room temperature)

Strawberry Swiss meringue buttercream
300g egg whites (8/9 large eggs)
375g caster sugar
675g soft unsalted butter
Strawberry coulis
1 tsp vanilla extract

You will need an electric mixer for
your cake and buttercream.

> *Swiss meringue buttercream, strawberry coulis and strawberry syrup can be made up to five days in advance and kept in sealed containers in the fridge. You can also substitute the strawberry filling, coulis and syrup with strawberry jam, maybe a lovely homemade one*

Method

For the strawberry shortbread biscuit, cream the butter and sugar until light and fluffy. In a separate bowl, sift together the flour, cornflour and salt. Add it to the butter and sugar mixture. Then using your fingers rub together until you have a rough breadcrumb consistency. Gently work through the freeze-dried strawberries.

Tip the mixture onto a clean work surface and use your hands to gently bring it together into a ball. Flatten slightly with the palm of your hand, wrap in cling film and place it in the fridge for 15 mins to firm..

Cut out three pieces of parchment the same size as your baking sheet. Place one onto the baking sheet and use the other two to roll out the dough. Remove the dough from the fridge and place it in between the parchment sheets. Gently roll the dough to about 5mm thick. Using one of the cake tins as a template cut out a circle and some biscuit shapes for decoration and carefully transfer them to your baking sheet. Bring the remaining dough together roll out again to make more biscuit shapes. If you want your biscuits to stand upright on your cake carefully push half of a toothpick into the bottom of biscuit.

Put the baking sheet into the fridge for 10mins to firm up again. This stops the biscuits from spreading. Pre-heat the oven to 180°C/160°C Fan. Bake the biscuits for 10-12 mins until they are lightly brown. Leave on the baking tray to cool.

For the strawberry filling, coulis and syrup, put the strawberries, sugar and lemon juice into a pan and stir. Bring to a boil, then turn the heat down and simmer gently for five mins. Remove the pan from the heat. Tipping the pan over a bowl use the back of a spoon to gently press down on the strawberries to collect the juice. This will be used as a syrup to soak the cake. Set aside to cool. Divide the remaining strawberries into three. Set aside two thirds to fill the cake and push the remaining third through a sieve to make a coulis. This will be added to the buttercream. Set aside to cool. If you are using jam instead of strawberries you may need a little boiling water to thin the juice down.

For the cake, grease and line 3 x 15cm sandwich tins with parchment and pre-heat your oven to 180°C/160°C fan. Place the bowl onto your weighing scales and reset. Crack the eggs into the bowl and note the weight. In separate bowls weigh out the butter, sugar and flour to the same weight as your eggs. All four ingredients should weigh the same.

Place an empty bowl onto your weighing scales and bring them back to zero. Crack the eggs into the bowl and note the weight. In separate bowls weigh out your butter, sugar and flour to the same weight as your eggs (all four ingredients should weigh the same)

Cream the butter and sugar until they are light and fluffy. Gradually beat in the eggs one at a time, making sure each one is incorporated before adding the next one. Sift together the flour & baking powder and with your mixer on a low speed gradually add to the creamed butter mixture.
Do not overbeat the mixture. Finally, add the milk and vanilla.
Divide the batter between the cake tins and bake for 25 mins or until a skewer inserted into the centre of the cakes comes out nice and clean. Cool in the baking tins for 10 mins before turning out onto a wire tray to cool completely.

For the Strawberry Swiss meringue buttercream.

Pop the egg whites and sugar into a heatproof bowl and set it over a saucepan of simmering water making sure the bottom of the bowl is not touching the water.

Gentle whisk the egg whites and sugar until the mixture has reached 70°C. If you don't have a thermometer whisk for a least 5 mins. After 5 mins rub a little of the mixture between two fingers - all the sugar should have dissolved. Remove the bowl from the heat.

Using a whisk attachment and a low speed whisk for 3-4 mins then increase the speed to medium and whisk until stiff peaks form. The meringue should be fluffy and glossy and cooled down.

With your mixer on medium speed add the butter one small spoonful at a time, ensuring that each spoonful is fully incorporated into the meringue before adding the next. During this process the meringue will collapse and look curdled but keep adding the butter until it is all incorporated and the meringue looks smooth and silky. Add the vanilla extract.

Scrape down the sides of the bowl and change to a paddle attachment (if you are using an electric mixer follow the instruction without changing the attachment). With your mixer on a slow speed continue beating for a further 10 mins.

Take half of the buttercream out of the bowl and set aside for the top coat of your cake. Add your strawberry coulis to the remaining buttercream and continue beating for a further few mins. If your buttercream looks a little runny then pop it into the fridge for 5-10 mins to firm up a little. Keep an eye on it though as you don't want it to get cold and firm up too much.

Assembling your cake.

If you are using pre-made buttercream this must be brought back to room temperature first. It will also need to be whisked for about 5 mins (it will go through the curdled stage again but don't worry - it will come back to its right consistency).

If possible, assemble the cake on a cake board, if not use a flat plate. Lightly infuse the three cake layers with the strawberry syrup using a pastry brush. Crumb coat and fill the cake with the strawberry buttercream. Then place the shortbread circle on the cake board and dab small amounts of buttercream over it and place the first layer of cake on top.

Spread about four heaped dessert spoons of the buttercream on top of the first layer of cake. Then gently spread half of the strawberries on top of the buttercream. Be careful not to go too near the edge of the cake as it will spill out when you add the next layer. Repeat with your second layer of cake, then top with the third layer.

Spread a thin layer of the buttercream on the top and round the sides of the cake, this locks in all the crumbs ready for the top coat. Pop the cake into the fridge for at least 30 mins to allow the buttercream to firm up.

Topcoat your cake with the vanilla buttercream. Spread a thick layer over the top and sides of the cake and smooth with a palette knife. Leave some buttercream for piping. Spoon some of the buttercream into a piping bag with a nozzle and decorate the top of the cake. Arrange the biscuits on the top and sides of the cake (you may need to dab a little of the buttercream onto the back of the side biscuits to help keep them in place). Finally, place a few strawberries on top.

JOBO BAKES

Apple sponge cake with brown butter Swiss meringue buttercream

This cake celebrates the delicious apples which are grown in abundance across Kent

Ingredients

For the cake
225g unsalted butter (room temp)
350g dark brown sugar
175g caster sugar
425g plain flour
325g eggs (6 large) - beaten
237ml sour cream (room temp)
1 tsp cinnamon
½ tsp bicarbonate of soda
¼ tsp salt

Dehydrated apple slices
1 apple

Brown butter
380g unsalted butter

Brown butter Swiss meringue buttercream
200g Egg whites (approx. 5/6 large eggs, room temp)
250g Caster sugar
Brown butter (room temp)

Apple compote and syrup
250g peeled, cored and diced eating apples (about 3 apples)
2 tbsp soft brown sugar
½ tsp cinnamon
1 star anise (optional)
3 tbsp water

You will need a stand or electric mixer for your cake and buttercream.

> *Dehydrated apples slices need to be prepared six-eight hours in advance. Brown butter, Swiss meringue buttercream, apple compote and apple syrup can be made up to five days ahead and kept in sealed containers in the fridge*

Method

Grease and line 3 x 20cm sandwich tins with parchment. Pre-heat your oven to 165°C/145°C fan.

Cream the butter and both sugars until they are light and fluffy. Beat in the eggs, one at a time making sure each one is incorporated into the mixture before adding the next one.

In a separate bowl sift the flour, cinnamon and salt and mix together. Gently mix the sour cream and bicarbonate of soda in another bowl.

Using a low speed gradually add ⅓ of the flour mixture into the creamed butter mixture followed by ½ of the sour cream mixture. Repeat this process again starting and finishing with the flour. Do not overbeat the mixture.

Divide the batter between the cake tins and put them in the oven straight away. Don't leave the mixture to stand, as the chemical reaction in the mixture starts to work as soon as the ingredients are combined, so they need to be in the oven to work their magic!

Bake for 20-25 mins until a skewer inserted into the centre of the cakes comes out clean or the mixture starts to come away from the side of the baking tins.

Leave the cakes in the tins for 10 mins before turning them out onto a wire tray to cool.

For the brown butter Swiss meringue buttercream, put the egg whites and sugar into a heatproof bowl and set it over a saucepan of simmering water. Make sure the bottom of the bowl is not touching the water.

Whisk the egg whites and sugar until the mixture has reached 70°C. If you don't have a thermometer whisk for a least 5 mins (rub the mixture between two fingers to make sure all the sugar has dissolved), remove the bowl from the heat.

Whisk the meringue on a low speed for 3-4 mins, then increase the speed to medium until stiff peaks form, the meringue is fluffy and glossy, and the bowl has completely cooled down.

Keeping the whisk on medium speed add the brown butter one small spoonful at a time. Ensure that each spoonful is fully incorporated into the meringue before adding the next. During this process the meringue will collapse and look curdled but keep adding the brown butter until it is all incorporated and the meringue looks smooth and silky.

Scrape down the sides of the bowl and change to the paddle attachment (if you are using an electric mixer carry on with the whisks). Continue on a slow speed and whisk for a further 10 mins. If your buttercream looks a little runny put it into the fridge for 5-10 mins to firm up a little. Keep an eye on it though as you don't want it to get cold and firm up too much.

For the dehydrated apple slices, which are optional, pre-heat your oven to its lowest temperature (about 40°C). Wash the apple and slice it as thinly as possible. If you want to add some colour to your apple dilute a small amount of colour with a little water and soak your apple slices for a few mins. Lay your apple slices directly onto the wire rack in your oven and dehydrate for six to eight hours.

For the brown butter, put the butter into a saucepan with a light coloured bottom (if you use a dark bottom saucepan you won't be able to see the colour of the butter as it browns). Melt the butter gently on a medium heat, stirring a couple of times. Once melted reduce the heat to low and simmer for about 5 mins until the butter has turned golden-brown colour.
Remove the pan from the heat and transfer the brown butter including all the sediments into a heatproof bowl. Set aside until cool..

For the apple compote and syrup put the diced apple into a small pan with the other ingredients. Stir and bring to a simmer. Put the lid on the pan and gently cook for 5 mins. Remove from the heat and strain the apple compote collecting the juice into a separate bowl to be used to make the apple syrup. Remove the star anise and set the compote aside to cool.
To make the syrup, add boiled water to the apple juice until you have two/three tbsp of apple syrup. Set aside to cool.

Assembling your cake.
If you are using premade buttercream this must be brought back to room temperature and will also need to be whisked for about 5mins (it may curdle briefly but don't worry as it will come back to the right consistency). If possible, assemble your cake onto a cake board if not use a flat plate.
Using a pastry brush lightly infuse the three cake layers with the apple syrup. Spread about 5 heaped dessert spoons of the buttercream on the top of the first layer of cake, then gently spread half of the apple compote on top of the buttercream. Repeat this process with the second layer of cake. Top off the cake with the third layer and more buttercream. Decorate the top of the cake with the apple slices.

Cheese in Kent

By Emma Young
instagram.com/thecheeseexplorer

This was in the early 1990's before the explosion of British cheese. Alex James was still a full-time rock star and to my knowledge there was no cheese made in Kent. How things have changed. You can now enjoy a full cheese board comprising of just cheese from Kent, covering a multitude of styles. Why not try one this evening with some delicious artisan bread and a Kentish wine to accompany them?

It's said that nowadays there are more cheeses made in Britain than in France. We are all familiar with traditional cheeses, such as Cheddar from the West Country, Stilton from Nottinghamshire, Wensleydale from Yorkshire as well as plenty from Sussex, Norfolk, Cornwall and even London. Whereas my lesser known home county, Kent - the Garden of England, has the space, countryside and the lush pastures perfect for grazing animals and therefore cheesemaking. So much so that there are currently around 40 dairy farms in Kent.

Dairy farming has been long established in the UK. Historically however the production of milk and cheese would remain localised to each farm. Farms would keep their own herds to provide milk and cheese for themselves. Any surplus would be sold very locally. The advent of the industrial revolution and subsequent railway network allowed for transportation of these cheeses to be sold to a wider market. This accessibility encouraged the growth of production.

Unfortunately the impact of two World Wars decimated cheese production. 'Government Cheddar' was the solution during these desperate times and consequently traditional cheesemaking became a memory. However, in the last few decades, cheese production has once more started flourishing. This growth has been organic and strong, as consumers' awareness and interest in local produce and provenance has similarly grown. The future is bright.

These are a few cheeses from Kent which you should try....

Winterdale Shaw

Winterdale Shaw is made by Winterdale Cheesemakers in Wrotham. It is made by Robin Betts and his team who also make Winterdale Oak Smoked Cheese.

The Betts family have been farming since 1946 however the cheesemaking side is a newer venture, an idea which was born by Robin and his wife Carla in 2000. By 2006, the idea had bloomed into a fully fledged dairy and their first cheese was produced in January of that year. The name Winterdale Shaw, as with many cheeses, is named after the place where it is made. A 'dale' is the old Kentish name for an open-ended valley. Winterdale is a valley there which remains open all the way to the Thames Estuary. Shaw is the name for an ancient woodland, much like the copse of oak trees where the dairy is set.

Winterdale Shaw is essentially a Cheddar. The family own their herd of around 100 Friesians and the life of Winterdale Shaw begins with their unpasteurised milk, straight from the milking parlour.

Once the curd is formed, it is put into cheese moulds and then pressed by beautiful traditional wooden cheese presses for 3 days. After pressing, the cheeses are wrapped in cotton muslin and matured for 10 months in a cave in the North Downs.

The Betts really capture the essence of their part of Kent in their cheese. You have the name and the geography behind it setting the scene. Their cows graze on the lush meadows of the chalky North Downs and some say, in a similar comparison to terroir in wine, that this imparts unique flavours to the milk which subsequently characterises their cheese. Finally, the finished cheeses are matured within the North Downs in a purpose-built cave where the flavour development continues to the end of the process.

Their cheese is carbon neutral, but what does this mean? They use minimal intervention of energy to make and sell their cheese. The milk is taken straight from the parlour to the dairy. By the time it reaches the dairy it is at around 32 deg C. This is the temperature needed to make the cheese so no energy is needed to heat it. The dairy employs solar panels and a ground heat pump to raise the temperature for scalding, while the cheese is matured in caves at a natural temperature. Even deliveries are made with an electric car. Completely carbon neutral!

Winterdale Shaw is smooth and creamy with earthy flavours, a good bite and a long finish.

Kentish Blue

Kentish Blue is an unpasteurised blue cheese made by Kingcott Cheese just outside Staplehurst. It is made by Steve and Karen Reynolds on their family run farm using unpasteurised milk from their herd of pedigree Friesians and Viking Red cows. The farm is in the process of switching over to Viking Red cattle as they believe the breed to be stronger and better suited to their farming methods and feed. The farm was purchased back in 1990 and in 2009 they started to add value to their raw product by manufacturing cheese. Last year in 2018 saw the introduction of a second cheese, Kingcott Blue.

At Kingcott Cheese, similarly to Winterdale, the cows are just around the corner from the dairy ensuring that the milk is at the correct temperature necessary for cheesemaking, with no need to re-heat the milk. The starter culture and vegetarian rennet are added to the milk to begin the process. Once set, long knives are used to cut the curd. Subsequently, the curds are ladled into moulds and after a few weeks they are ready to be pierced to commence the blue veining growth. After 2 ½ -3 months of careful affinage, the cheeses are ready to be released to the world! Flavours are mellow and saline with a gentle vegetal bitter aftertaste. The texture and flavour varies from a very slight crumble and higher acidity in younger batches to smooth, mushroomy and buttery textures in those which are slightly more aged.

Graceburn

Graceburn cheese is made by Blackwood's Cheese Company in Edenbridge. Dave Holton and Tim Jarvis head the team along with their new apprentice who started with them just this year. Founded just 6 years ago in 2013, Blackwoods make unpasteurised, soft, cow's milk cheese using milk from Commonwork Organic Farm. The milk is collected directly as the cows are being milked.

The herd consists of Holstein Friesians, Swedish Reds and Montbeliardes, bred in. The Swedish Red cows milk improves the butterfat content, whereas the Montbeliarde milk raises the overall protein content and make excellent cheese. The same breed is used throughout France, particularly in the Savoie and Franche-Comté departments. The Blackwood's herd is just around the corner from the dairy and the Blackwoods team pride themselves on using as little intervention as possible. Dave originally learnt cheesemaking in Australia before moving to London, where he took up a job as a Neal's Yard Dairy Christmas temp and ended up staying! He furthered his trade in the maturing rooms, working on affinage as well as a stint at Mons Fromager Affineur in St Haon le Chatel in the Loire department of France. Tim started in the cheese industry as a Wholesale Cheesemonger before joining Blackwoods in 2013.

Graceburn is a based on a Persian fetta style cheese; a style which Dave learnt how to make in Australia. This is a lot smoother in texture and flavour than the better known Greek Feta PDO. The cheese is marinated in extra virgin olive oil and rapeseed oil, while a blend of garlic, thyme, bay and pepper are used to add flavour. I am never without a jar of Graceburn in my fridge. The cheese is so versatile – you can crumble it into salads, into pastries, onto soups and sometimes I just find myself eating it with a fork. The marinade is a perfect balance of all the herbs and spices and although flavoured, it is subtle enough not to completely overwhelm.

Blackwood's also make a few other lactic cows milk cheeses namely Edmund Tew and William Heaps. The former is made in the style of the French cheese, Langres, and William Heaps is a fresh lactic cheese, which they sometimes decorate seasonally with wildflowers and wild garlic. I have enjoyed watching the Edmund Tew recipe changing colour and form over the last couple of years, as they perfect their recipe.

Dave and Tim are great cheesemakers who are constantly improving their cheesemaking skills through courses or simply experimenting in the dairy. While keeping to the traditional rules of cheesemaking they are willing to innovate with recipes and techniques to improve current products.

Fremlin's Kentish Log

Fremlin's Kentish Log is an unpasteurised goats cheese made by Ellie's Dairy in the North Downs. It is one of the newer cheeses in the Ellie's Dairy range, all of which are unpasteurised goats cheeses. It is a bloomy rinded, large format goat log. The cheese takes its name from the herd's chief male goat, Fremlin.

Ellie's Dairy was founded in 2004 by owners David Shannon and Debbie Vernon. They have a herd of around 300 pedigree dairy goats which produce the high quality unpasteurised goats milk that is used in their cheeses. Ellie's dairy is an ethical supplier for several reasons. The welfare of their goats is paramount. They are not certified organic by choice, but they may as well be, following their ethics and practises. They work closely with each animal and their differing strengths and personalities. This level of attention is illustrated by the age of some of their herd. In 'normal' dairy goat farms the oldest goats are usually around 5 years old but David and Debbie have goats as old as 11-12 years. Their herd have access to grazing all year round. They are pasture fed but can come and go to a nearby large barn when they need more shelter.

During the winter months in the barn they are fed hay from the farm's meadows. Cereals top up their diet when it is necessary. These cereals are grown by a local farmer who holds dear the same values as Ellie's Dairy. The combination of this local feed, the wildflowers in the meadow and the milk remaining unpasteurised leads to a beautiful complexity in the milk and cheese, which is not apparent in pasteurised alternatives. Nothing is wasted at Ellie's Dairy. The male goats are raised alongside the females, until the strongest are selected to continue as their breeding males. The rest are not simply culled, their meat is sold to restaurants and their skins to a tannery to make rugs.

Ellie's Dairy make a variety of styles and flavours of cheese. However, one of the best, Fremlin's Kentish Log is smooth and silky in texture with lactic flavours and a pronounced lemon finish.

Ashmore Kentish Cheese

Ashmore Kentish cheeses are made by Cheesemakers of Canterbury, in Faversham. The company was established in 2007 by Jane Bowyer, who already had 20 years of experience in the industry. She saw a gap in the market for unpasteurised, natural rinded cheeses in Kent. With a stroke of luck a cheesemaking couple in Wiltshire who were planning on retiring, passed on their skills, equipment and even the recipe for Ashmore cheese. According to their website the cheese started life in a smallholders' text book written by the North of Scotland College of Agriculture! Cheesemakers of Canterbury now make many adaptations of the recipe, as well as some more esoteric recipes, such as Bowyer's Brie, Chaucer's Camembert and Dargate Dumpy Ewe's milk cheese.

Ashmore Farmhouse is the original recipe which is an unpasteurised, natural rinded cheddar style, which originates from a Friesian herd. After making the curd, the cheeses are wrapped in cotton muslin and pressed in traditional 19th century presses for a couple of days. Unusually they are unwrapped before they are placed on pine shelves and matured for a minimum of 5 months, where they are turned daily.

Flavours are warm and cooked with a good acidity and length. It is a great cheese to pair with chutneys such as caramelised onion and mixed fruit chutneys.

Kentish Oils

kentishcondiments.com

One of the great pleasures of spring is viewing the bright yellow rapeseed crops growing, signifying the start of warmer weather and longer days. Vast acres have been given over to this crop in the past 10 years, as farmers have realised the value their small dark seeds bring. For decades the seeds where heat pressed and made into nondescript vegetable oils but there has been a huge shift in production. Now, many are single estate and cold pressed to produce a golden oil that has found popularity amongst some of the top chefs in the country. It is not hard to see why given its versatility and sought after properties. It is high in mono-unsaturated fats (half the saturated fat of Olive Oil) and can be heated to a far higher temperature without spoiling it's antioxidant properties or character. This makes it a healthier and more practical option for cooking with and one of the prime reasons it has exploded in popularity. It's high Omega 3 and 6 content, which are said to help prevent against heart disease and have anti-inflammatory properties, have further fuelled the nations desire for this home grown oil.

One of the best-known independent producers of Rapeseed Oil is Kentish Oils. Owned by Laura Bounds, the brand has grown significantly since it's launch 10 years ago. This is largely a result of Laura's passion for the oil which is evident when you speak with her. Her drive for excellence is very much paramount to Kentish Oils success and why so many chefs are using her oils.

The seeds Kentish Oils use are from specially selected crops, grown in East Kent before being cold pressed at their purpose built unit near Bridge in Canterbury. The oils are made in small batches by hand with 100% traceability from seed to bottle providing solid provenance. In the past few years Laura has incorporated a range of flavourings to her oils making them ideal for dressings. The most recent being Garden Mint, Basil and Rosemary which can transform a boring salad into something far more delectable.

Kentish Oils are widely available throughout Kent alongside their range of delicious mayonnaise.

The Wonky Parsnip

thewonkyparsnip.com

Growing your own veg is a wonderful thing. We only have a moderate garden at home but have 4 dedicated raised beds, each measuring X by X where we grow a range of vegetables that taste so good!. For those with large families to feed (like my project manager Sam), then using a local supplier of veg boxes could be really beneficial, especially if those boxes might contain some weird and wonderful produce such as South African gem squash or Red sweetcorn. This is exactly what you can find from the Wonky Parsnip. In fact Laura Brady, the owner, told me that "we think of ourselves as providing you exotic produce locally grown".

Here in Kent we are lucky to have a fairly warm climate and mostly flat land with chalky sub rock. This allows for a diverse range of farming activities. From arable cropping, such as wheat and barley to fruit and fresh produce, as well as hops and livestock. Having worked in most of these areas I decided it was time to combine my knowledge of agriculture and start my own venture. Growing produce in Kent is great as London is nearby and we have a huge array of superb restaurants in Kent with chefs championing local produce. I might only have a one acre patch but I grow over 150 varieties of unusual fruits and vegetables. Everything is either propagated in my greenhouse or directly sown using a hand seed drill.

Specialising in growing weird and wonderful fruit and vegetables is great fun allowing for a diverse crop. I spent a lot of time scouring through traditional seed catalogues, as well as searching online for produce you don't often see, which may adapt well in Kent. The range is extraordinary; anything from a black or striped radish to things such as Mexican tomatiolos, the ingredient used in authentic salsa. Then there is the cucamelon. A grape sized cucumber with the striping of a watermelon. Neither are very common in the UK but we have found ways to grow them well here in the Kentish climate!

It's vital to keep an eye on food trends to anticipate what will be popular in the coming season. It's always a matter of trial and error. Some things work and some things don't. The summer of 2018 proved particularly challenging as flea beetles thrived, destroying most brassica crops such as pac choi, mustards and radishes. We also didn't have rain for six weeks, so we had to re-sow a lot of crops with ones that could better survive the dry conditions. With ever changing seasons and climate change this will be common thinking across most farms, where it's now necessary to change varieties to suit the climate. This has been well illustrated in Kent, where we have seen flourishing grape production due to our increased summer temperatures, as well as our chalky soils making perfect conditions for grape production.

Growing on just one acre we have produced 10,000's of kg of produce in just one season. With all our jobs done by hand, we seed intensively as soon as a crop is finished. We then replant that area with another crop from a different plant family that will complement the crops growing on either side. For example, the rotation may be rainbow carrots, sprouting cauliflowers followed by brown fennel. We also only plant small blocks of each crop but these blocks are planted multiple times across a field. This is done to minimise the risk of pest damage and the spread of disease.

Biddenden Vineyards

biddendenvineyards.com

If you have lived in Kent for any amount of time you would be hard pressed to not be aware of Biddenden wines and ciders. I first discovered their cider at the Smarden Bell where it was served in half pints circa 1990. As students, it not only provided amazing quality, but also great value given it's alcohol content. The added benefit being that my friend, Ruan, and I always seemed to get invited to a party after closing time. I don't really recall too much about them…

Biddenden of course is not only famed for its cider, available in a multitude of styles, but for its wines and in particular the Ortega. First planted in 1969 they have been a driving force in the UK's wine landscape ever since.

Biddenden Vineyards was founded in 1969 by current owner Julian Barnes's family. Planting commenced in 1969 but it was not until 1972 that Ortega was planted for the first time, which has gone on to become the vineyards signature varietal and now accounts for 50% of all plantings.

Of course the viticultural landscape in Kent (and the UK) has changed beyond recognition since those early days. Would anyone, even in the 1990's predict that traditional French Champagne houses would be buying up vast plots of land to plant with vines? As Julian quite rightly says, 'It is a great endorsement.'
Having such experience brings its benefits. For example, having a comprehensive knowledge of the vines' needs throughout the season. This enables Julian to feed the vines the nutrients they need at the time they need them most. An understanding reached through the time and experience of many UK wine seasons.

It's also a great industry to be working in. Not only friendly but with a cacophony of artistic and social types, who all bring their own history and entrenerpreship. It is a small world, as they say.

The endless summer of 2018 has provided grapes with sugar levels that they could only dream of, so I for one am particularly looking forward to tasting the wines. The cellar door is the place to do this as you occasionally find some wines that are only available there as production is so low. And then only in certain years. Perhaps for me the most interesting of these is the Pinot Noir, which is produced where there has been a sufficiently large crop of the desired quality that it is not needed for the sparkling wines, in which it is an integral component. Julian is not trying to make a Burgundian wine, but one from Kent, letting its natural flavours shine through by ageing in steel as opposed to oak.

Cider is an integral part of the business and one that has been in production since the late 1970's. I have fond memories of enjoying it at the Smarden Bell in the early 1990's where it was restricted to half pints at a time due to its strength. I recall that every visit to this pub ended up as a house party (closing time was 11:00pm then if you remember).

Six apple varieties are grown here for apple juice of which two really stand out for their point of difference. The Red Love is only available here commercially and has red skin and flesh. Originally developed in Switzerland over 25 years by Markus Kobelt it is sweet yet tangy making it perfect for a stand alone drink or to be enjoyed in a cocktail. The other is H** which literally the size of a human head.

Investment in the apple juice side of the business has been substantial recently with a new belt press introduced increasing production times so minimising oxidation. Much like wine, a cross flow filtration system has been put into place and a stelvin closure for the juices being the first in the UK to do so.

Spiced cider with gammon or pork

Ingredients
2kg piece uncooked plain ham, boned, rolled and tied
750ml Spiced Biddenden Cider
10 black peppercorns
Pinch of sea salt
1 tbsp demerara sugar (for the glaze)

Method
Soak the gammon for at least 3 hours or overnight in water in your fridge.
Put the gammon with all the ingredients in a large pot ensuring the liquid covers meat. If not add some apple juice or water. Bring this to boil then reduce the heat and simmer gently for 75 mins turning the gammon every 25 mins or so.
Carefully take out the gammon and place on a roasting tray. Trim off the fat and score the gammon with a sharp knife in a hexagonal pattern.

Make a glaze by putting a ladle full of the cooking liquid in a fresh pan and adding the sugar. Reduce until it takes on a glaze like consistency and pour over the gammon. Place in the oven for 15 mins until browned then serve.

Sylvia & Terry Chocolates

sylviaandterry.com

If asked, most people enjoy chocolate, perhaps the most pleasurable of all comfort foods. Sadly the raw cacao beans that are processed to make chocolate, have to be imported to make this most wonderful of treats. Chocolate lines countless supermarket aisles in various guises from confectionary, cereals, patisserie, and liquors to a vast array of cakes. It is all too easy to buy from well known commercial brands, less so from smaller independent artisan local producers. Based near the Kent coast, Sylvia and Terry Chocolates are one such producer who incorporate Kentish produce into their chocolates.

Growing cacao trees in the UK is not impossible, but due to the notoriously difficult nature of growing them, especially for commercial purposes, it might as well be. Found in tropical climates such as Central and South America, West Africa or the Caribbean, the trees are simply not suited to our climate. The trees natural pollination is from insects, which do not live in Europe, meaning each tree has to be pollinated by hand. The difficulty of this undertaking is compounded by the flowers only lasting for one solitary day. The trees need plenty of rain and 100% humidity, while the fact that each tree produces only 1000 cocoa beans per year, equating to roughly 1kg of chocolate, means it is simply unviable to grow them here.

Despite the problems (the trees only produce their small pumpkin like pods that hold the beans for around 25 years and dislike direct sunlight) they are grown in a 1000 square meter facility near Reading called the International Cocoa Quarantine Centre. The centre exists primarily to preserve the species, which are highly susceptible to disease. Having no naturally occurring diseases in the UK, they ensure the species survival should anything catastrophic happen. The cultivated plants are then transported around the world disease free.

Sylvia and Terry chocolates are available to purchase directly from their website.

Q. Tell me about flavour development and ideas?
A. We make classic chocolates using, wherever possible, classic English and Kentish flavours. Sometimes we add a new twist or pair with a modern flavour. I look back to the treats I enjoyed in my childhood, often reinventing old favorites with gourmet ingredients. Orchard fruits, herbs and floral notes form the foundation of our flavours, which we believe gives our products real Kentish flavour.

Flavour development always starts with a solid foundation from a tried and tested recipe. Chocolate making is a science and you have to understand the interaction of ingredients in a chocolate before you can start inventing your own combinations. Once you have that foundation under your belt, you can experiment by carefully tweaking recipes and creating your own combinations. This is by no means a quick process and it typically takes many adjustments before the balance is right.

Q. Have you had a great idea and it turned out to be horrible?
A. Not one of my ideas but a customer did once request a series of bespoke savoury macarons. They were certainly not the most delicious things we have ever made! They fitted the brief and the client was very happy, but the tomato ketchup macaron is something I'd rather not eat again!

Q. What ingredients do you source from Kent?
A. As much as we can. Orchard fruits such as quince, damson, plum, apple and pear, as well as berries in season. We use lots and lots of Kentish cobnuts and local beer, wine, cider, liqueurs and juices.

Q. How did you learn to temper the chocolate and how long did it take?
A. A great friend of mine, Jean-Michel Vilain, a master French baker and pâtissier taught me the basics in his bakery many years ago. Since then I have trained in various chocolate academies, so the development of my skill is always ongoing. There is always something to learn and perfect. Tempering chocolate is a really tricky thing to master as it depends upon so many variables, such as room temperature and humidity. It took me a good two years to really master the skill and be able to troubleshoot a problem and fix it before you have ruined a batch of bonbons.

Q. Which other chocolatiers do you admire and why?
A. I admire Willie Pike, I'm sure I am not alone in this. He is one of the worlds great teachers and inspires everyone who has the pleasure to be trained by him. I attended a short chocolate course with him in Scotland before I started Sylvia and Terry. He has devoted much of his career to inspiring and supporting people starting off in the business.

Q. What is the best part of your job?
A. Eating a lot of chocolate! Watching other people eating and enjoying our creations and especially sharing stories of our childhood experiences of chocolate and family favourites. It brings people together.

Q. Do you have any interesting fact or anecdotes about your chocolates.
A. We have sent our chocolates across the globe. We once delivered 10,000 chocolates to the Ritz which were flown to Bahrain for a very special wedding.

Q. How time consuming is it to make chocolates?
A. Very! To craft and perfect a chocolate from start to finish is a process of three days.

139

Woodchurch Wines

woodchurchwine.co.uk

You would be hard pressed to have missed the influx of English vineyards over the past decade, especially in Kent. To me, being an ex-sommelier, fine wine merchant and wine writer it brings a lot of happiness. Few things beat driving or cycling through the countryside, with far-reaching vistas of vineyards during July and August. It just seems magical to me. As the vines mature the views will become more spectacular and hopefully not hidden behind hedges, rendering them invisible. For me, this is one of the main differences between us and the Continent - the absence of hedgerows.

We are privileged to have more than 50 vineyards in Kent which we can be proud of. To me, it makes total sense to serve a wine from Kent to any fortunate guests you are hosting, maybe without telling them what it is, and gauging their opinion? To make your experience even more enjoyable, why not visit the vineyard first to sample the wines and chat with the winemaker? A word of warning; just because there is a beautiful building or visitors centre it does not automatically mean the wine is excellent. I have been impressed by the quality of some, yet sorely disappointed by others...

Woodchurch for me is one of the best, and I have loved their wines since my first visit three years ago. Set in a stunning location with far-reaching views across the flats of Romney Marsh to the coast, it is superbly situated and it was a must to include them in this book.

Q. How did you select the site for Woodchurch Wines?
A. We spent nearly a year searching for the land for our vineyard. We had several essential criteria so it was a difficult process finding the right spot. The site at Woodchurch met our key requirements, so we had a soil survey to check the land was suitable for vines. A few adjustments to the soil and site were required but we now feel very lucky we were able to create the vineyard on such a beautiful spot.

Q. When did you plant the vines and what was that process like?
A. We planted in 2009. I remember the day very well. It was very stressful and exciting all at the same time. We hired a company from Germany, who come to the UK every year with a special vine planting machine. It is guided by lasers to ensure the vines are planted in exactly the right place. It creates a deep channel in the ground, then plants a vine and finally closes up the channel behind it. It was then just left for us to go back through the vineyard to push in a supporting steel cane and place a tube over the vine to protect it from rabbits!

Q. What was the first bottle of your own wine that you opened? Did you make an occasion of it?
A. The first bottle we opened was a 2012 Classic Cuvée. It was just the two of us and we couldn't have been more thrilled. We were so proud of ourselves for producing our first wine!

Q. Where did you learn about wine?
A. We both completed various viticulture and wine courses, including courses at Plumpton College.

Q. Apart from your own wine, what do you enjoy drinking?
A. We always enjoy trying other wines from the UK. It is lovely to be part of this exciting, new developing industry.

Q. What food would you pair your wines with?
A. We recommend pairing the Classic Cuvée with fish dishes. For example, one of our recommended dishes is Dover sole and caper sauce. Our rosé is a perfect Summer party aperitif but it also goes well with salmon starters and desserts. It pairs particularly well with Eton Mess. Our Blanc de Blancs goes well with many seafood and chicken dishes however our favourite pairing is with crab cakes.

Q. Last year was a bumper harvest and exceptional vintage. Will you make a special Cuvée at all?
A. All of our wine is vintage, so as with other years we are producing three sparkling wines from the 2018 harvest. A Classic Cuvée, a Rosé and a Blanc de blancs. We've also produced some still Chardonnay and Pinot Noir. It was an outstanding year and it's no big surprise that all of the wines are tasting delicious in tank. We're hoping for some outstanding wines as a result.

Q. What is the future looking like for wineries in Kent and why?
A. Kent is a great place to grow vines and produce quality ripe fruit. The consistent warm, dry summers are perfect for grape growing. We have some amazing producers close by making world class wines. The Champagne house Taittinger has recently planted vines in Kent, which certainly gives us confidence we're in the right area for grape growing!

Q. What are the nicest comments you have received about your wines?
A. As well as winning lots of international medals we have also received some excellent feedback from wine experts. Tom Stevenson, the world's leading authority on Champagne gave us some great feedback on all our wines but held back his highest praise to our Blanc de blancs. Our Rosé is a favourite of Matthew Jukes and it has featured in his English Wine Compendium. Recently we were also recommended by the Independent's food and wine writer, Terry Kirby.

Q. If you could have a second vineyard where would it be?
A. One vineyard is quite enough work for now! If we were to expand we would want to stay close to Woodchurch since we know the area is proven for producing fantastic wines.

Copper Rivet Distillery

coppperrivetdistillery.com

There are not many distilleries, breweries or wineries that have resonated with me as much as Copper Rivet, which has been established since 2016. They are doing exactly what I would love to do. Creating a product of exemplary quality and provenance with the utmost attention to detail. They examine each step for improvement to raise their benchmark even higher.

Housed in the magnificent Pumphouse No. 5, the distillery is adjacent to the River Medway. The site was a chance discovery. Matthew Russell, one of the family owners along with Stephen and Bob, had been visiting historic Upnor Castle, when they looked across the river and saw the Pumphouse. Striking while the iron was hot, Matthew drove to Chatham Maritime, the following Monday and discovered the building was for sale. Whether fate played a part I don't know but the family had been searching for a suitable property for this project as far afield as Scotland. So to find one, which fitted the bill so perfectly and in their home town was truly fortunate.

After extensive planning the brothers finally acquired Pumphouse No 5 in 2015. Local craftsmen were commissioned to build the 10m column still, which would produce their own Neutral Grain Spirit (NGS). NGS is a common product in Scotland but almost unheard of in England. 99.9% of distillers buy in their NGS (presumably of varying quality) in plastic containers to convert into their own brands of gin.
Copper Rivet's passion for quality is extraordinary. They go to great lengths to ensure they control the process from growing the grain right through to bottling. It's a gamble that they are winning and one that results in a unique selling point. If a company is willing to go to these lengths, with care and consideration from the outset, then you can be certain that the finished product will be exemplary.

Their obsession for quality means they only use grains grown locally, enabling them to work in conjunction with the farmer to ensure the best quality. The three grains they use, wheat, barley and rye are milled on site and form the starting point for the production of their gin, vodka and whisky. Production is headed up by Abhi, who was recruited from the International Centre for Brewing and Distilling in Edinburgh, where he was teaching post graduates. He certainly had the technical skills required and shared the brothers passion. The fact that Abhi could also design the pump house must have been a very exciting proposition as well. Within it there are 3 stills names after family members:
Sandy – Named after the Russell's paternal grandfather which will be used for Whisky.
Joyce – Their grandmother who was tall and fiery which is used to make the NGS.
Janet – There maternal grandmother who was soft and delicate is used to distil the gin.

Dockyard Gin

Having taken so much care to create a spirit in-house, it is only reasonable to expect that when put through a unique copper still (made to their own specifications) that the final product should be exceptional. Abhi's design of the still is unique (patent pending). It enables Abhi to insert a cartridge containing a bouquet garni of aromatics to flavour the gin. These aromatics include Italian juniper berries, locally sourced elderflower, Bulgarian coriander seeds, Spanish orange peel, Italian lemon peel, Guatemalan green cardamom, grains of paradise from Africa, European angelica root and orris root.

With such a heady combination it's no surprise the final gin is so smooth and elegant that it can be sipped. It may be down to the time of year I visited but I found hints of Christmas cake in there, probably down to the citrus and spice. Maybe what makes the final product so special is that the maceration happens away from the heat source so is conducted at the same temperature. This allows subtle nuances to develop and aids to the smoothness.

Chatham has many maritime and military connections. Nelson learnt to sail there, the first Union Flag was produced there and Resolute Desk is in the Oval Office. So it was no wonder that as news spread about the sheer quality of Copper Rivet Dockyard gin, that it was requested for use in the naming ceremony for HMS Medway. The Royal Navy have launched more than 4000 ships yet this was only the second to be launched without champagne. The other was Elisabeth where a whisky was used.

Vela Vodka

I am not a regular vodka drinker as I generally like my spirits neat, full of flavour and character. However this charcoal filtered vodka is different. It has complex notes with a back note of pepper. I generally could drink this neat over ice with a splash of something like lime as they recommend. The vodka is named after the sail shaped constellation used for navigation since Roman times

Son of a Gun

This is a bit of a rarity, being the (unaged) young spirit that has been briefly cask aged and then charcoal filtered and which will ultimately be used for their whisky. I found a beautiful nuttiness to it complemented by flavours of pepper and honey. It has been distilled to be used in cocktails primarily. I witnessed the making of an Old Fashioned, using the spirit and angostura bitters. The mixologist must have spent five mins dissolving the sugar cube into the drink. Their dedication to perfection continues.

Copper Rivet is producing one of the very best gins in the UK and deliver on their promise. The future looks exciting with the release of a whisky in 2020. Perhaps more exciting for me, however are Copper Rivets experiments with terroir. They plan to produce gin from individual parcels of grain to determine if there is a difference. They will all be inoculated using Anchor Gold Yeast to retain consistency and then distilled in an identical fashion. This project is unique to Copper Rivet and offers a very exciting opportunity. I cannot wait to taste them.

Old Dairy Brewery

olddairybrewery.com

Beer has been produced in Kent for centuries, and we have an incredible heritage of hop growing in the county. The British Hop Association states on its website "The cultivation of hops was probably introduced from Flanders to England in the Maidstone area of Kent at the end of the 15th century". I have lived in Maidstone for most of my life but was unaware of this fact. Reading it did bring a smile to my face as I have a love for Flanders, where I have cycled hundreds of miles with my good friend David Vant. Nothing is finer after a hard ride ascending the cobbled and steep (bergs) hills than a glass of Belgium beer, and nothing more welcoming after a ride to the Kentish coast in summer than a pint of fine ale.

Kent now has more than 50 breweries which I feel we should all seek out. Why buy from the major brands when such good produce is available on our doorsteps? Unlike wine, beer is relatively inexpensive so we can experiment, try styles we are not familiar with The next time you are in the pub, ask for a local pint, or at least for a taste before you buy. Most good landlords will happily oblige and tell you about the beer.

Located in the beautiful town of Tenterden, the scene of many Saturday nights spent as a teenager consuming more real ale than is necessary with my friend Ruan, it is one of the most successful of the regional breweries. Not only is there a strong range of beers under the Old Dairy label, but also, since 2017 under a new brand called Cattle Shed. Cattle Shed was launched to produce less traditional styles, giving the multicultural team an opportunity to go "off-piste" I love this concept as for me beer is all about experimentation and flavour experiences. I caught up with Virginia, a long term member of staff and CAMRA member to find out more.

Q. Who comes up with the concepts of the beer labels?
A. As a team we collaborate to come up with ideas that respect our history. These ideas are then sent to a designer who articulates them into our labels. It is not always easy as we have a idea in our minds eye, but they are generally spot on at the first attempt. Add - The Old Dairy Team whether it be the brewing team or office staff, are all passionate about craft ales and this certainly shows in everything brewed.

Q. Being located in Tenterden, are most of your hops sourced from Kent?
A. We work very closely with Ross Hukins of Hukins Hops, who are just 3 miles away from the brewery. We buy as much as we can from him, but he cannot grow every variety that we need, so have to buy those in for elsewhere. For example the Uber has Citra and Chinnok in which he does not grow. A lot of the beers have Challenger, Fuggles, Goldings and Cascade in which he does.

Q. You make a Green Beer what is that?
A. Hops are picked in September and are usually sent to an oast house to be dried. We take a proportion of those hops (Bullion and Challenger) and make a single hop beer within 12 hours of them being picked. That is pretty unique and special to Kent as be have the access to the hops so quickly. This lends a very fresh and fruity flavour to the beers. Each beer is a one off so the cask beer is only available in September.

Q. What happens to the spent grain?
A. This is taken away to feed the cattle from which we also get milk as well.

Q. How much beer do you produce a year?
A. Compared to micro breweries we sell a lot, some 1m pints a year. But compare this to someone like Sharps, we are small. But our size also works to our advantage as we can be experimental with new beers and our staff are truly passionate and care as they know we are not a big business. What they do individually impacts the business and we our all on the same page in trying to make the best beer possible.

Q. What is the difference between a cask conditioned beer?
A. A cask beer can be the utopia of beer. It is beer that has been put in casks by the brewer unmolested and ready to undergo a secondary fermentation in the barrel. The beer evolves in the cask, lovingly look after by the pubs landlord until they deem it to be in perfect condition and ready to serve. Much like in Champagne, the yeasts are fuelled by the sugar turning the liquid into alcohol with a slight fizz.

Cellar management by the landlord is paramount to it turning into a good pint. Meticulous cleaning is essential and also maintaining the perfect cellar temperature. Once ready it needs to be enjoyed relatively quickly ensuring the hydraulic pumps are in frequent use. You do not want beer languishing in the pipes for too long.

Q. How have you seen the industry change since you started?
A. When I first worked for a brewery 20 years ago there were only eight breweries in Kent. Now, with all the micro breweries there must be more than 50, so an explosion of them making the market very competitive. Factor in that pubs are also closing at an alarming rate then it creates an interesting business environment. We look for different ways to differentiate ourselves and to win awards. Our Snow Top for example won CAMRA Champion Beer of Britain in 2016 which has a marked effect on consumer awareness and also sales.

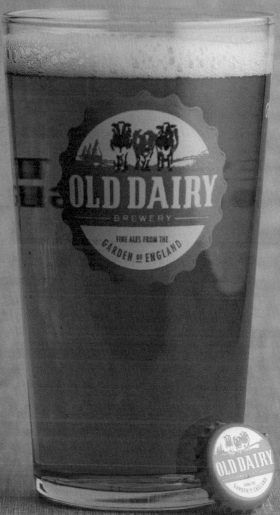

Cobnuts by Gilly Jones

kentishcobnutsassociation.org.uk

The Kentish Cobnut, a cultivated variety of hazelnut is traditionally grown in Kent and neighbouring counties. Their history goes back a long way but the first documented records are from the 17th century, when a drawing of a 'Cob Nut' was first published. Mr Lambert of Goudhurst bred the variety which we now know as the Kent Cob, (or Kentish Cob) in about 1830. You can still see his house near the church. Kent Cob is not the only variety: others include White Filbert – a very old, small and sweet variety, Ennis, Gunslebert, Cosford Cob and others. All these varieties are grown in Kent and neighbouring counties, while collectively known as cobnuts.

Traditionally they are grown in orchards or plats, as we like to call them here in Kent. Grown in rows, ten to twelve feet apart, and pruned annually to keep them at picking level and to promote an abundance of fruiting wood. In February, if you look closely, you will see the very tiny red star-like female flowers. The male catkins are easy to see as they open and turn yellow to release their pollen. Of course, there are not many insects around at this time of year for pollination but that's not a problem as the wind does the job, carrying the tiny pollen grains over great distances.

If you like your cobnuts crisp and crunchy it's worth getting your teeth into them as soon as picked, which is late August and into September. If you like them sweeter and more flavoursome, though with less of the crunch factor, then you will enjoy them later in September into October and even up to Christmas.

Cobnuts are valuable for their high nutritional content. They are high in Vitamin E, Vitamin B1, Vitamin B6 and calcium, with protein and fibre making up 12-17% of their volume.

How to eat these delicious and nutritious English cobnuts? You can take them out of their frilly husks, crack them and eat them fresh, either green and crunchy or golden and sweetly flavoursome. Traditionally they are eaten at the end of a meal to prolong the enjoyment, accompanied, perhaps, by a glass of port. Alternatively you can crack, chop and sprinkle them on autumn crumbles or use them in fruit tarts or savoury dishes; a favourite recipe is to sprinkle them over grilled trout instead of the usual flaked almonds.

Many more recipes are to be found on the web and the Kentish Cobnuts Association website in particular offers more suggestions (kentishcobnutsassociation.org.uk). However for sheer taste and enjoyment simply roasting them in the oven until lightly browned and served with a sprinkle of salt can't be beaten: the flavour is amazing!

These days cobnuts are enjoying a strong revival and you will find them headlining in any number of products such as preserves, oil and confectionary at farmers' markets and food fairs all over the south of England.

If you would like to try Gilly Jones's Cobnut and Bramley Apple Granola Muesli it can be found on her website along with other cobnut products at www.gillyjones.com

Spiced nut pilaf

2 tablespoons olive oil
100g (4oz) or more cobnuts, shelled and split.
2 red onions, chopped
1 dessert-spoonful grated root ginger
3 or 4 garlic cloves, chopped
225g (4oz) basmati rice
Seeds from 3 green cardamom pods
2 cinnamon sticks
100g (4oz) ready-to-eat-dried apricots, chopped
Approx 900 ml (1 ½ pints), hot vegetable stock or water
3 teaspoons honey
Grated zest 1 orange

Fry the nuts in the oil in a large frying pan until golden; or roast them.

Remove nuts from pan and fry the onions in the oil for 10-15 mins. Then add the ginger, garlic, rice and spices and stir fry for a few seconds.

Stir in the stock, apricots and honey, season to taste, then cover and simmer until the rice is cooked. Stir in the orange zest and the nuts and serve.

Based on a recipe by Janette Marshall.

Pure Kent Flour

purekent.wordpress.com/on-the-farm

Eckley Farms is just around the corner from Hush Heath Winery. The farm is run by Claire and Guy Eckley and they produce a wonderful stone-ground wholemeal flour that is used by bakeries in Kent and also available to purchase for home use. I met with Claire to discuss their flour.

Q. Tell me about the farm and how you came to be growing wheat? Have you always produced bread or is it a later addition to the farm?
A. My husband's family have been here since the 1950s, starting off as a mixed farm, with sheep, orchards, and hops. More recently in the '80s, there was a move to arable farming, such as crops you can harvest with a combine harvester. We've always grown milling varieties, which are aimed at bread-making, as they have a higher protein content. We find the soil here in the Weald of Kent really suited to growing these varieties and they command a premium for us. This enables us to get a little extra money when we sell to places like Kingsmill and Warburtons. However we decided we wanted to mill some of the flour ourselves on the farm. We wanted to be able to supply local flour to local bakers in Kent, so that they could make a Kent loaf. We don't mill very much. Overall we grow about 2500-3000 tons of wheat a year that goes into U.K. bread-making, while we keep back two to three tons for milling ourselves.

That really is a tiny quantity.
It is a tiny amount but of course we're selling it at a much increased price, which is great for us as farmers who are trying to add value to our produce. After we've harvested it we clean the crop, to make sure there's no bugs and stones in the wheat, and then we mill it on our wooden mill that we brought in from Austria.

The mill still looks brand new even though it's five years old. It's beautifully made in pine. It looks absolutely exquisite. It's almost like a piece of art, I think. Very different from the windmills I've seen in Holland and in Belgium. It looks very beautiful, very artisan, and I love it!

The mill is a real piece of craftsmanship. It is made by factories in the Austrian Alps, using the local Alpine pine, while the milling stones are composite, so they're set in concrete. Maybe a little less romantic but it's been a tradition for the past 50 or 60 years. They come in all sizes, so you can even get one that fits on your kitchen work surface. As we are a commercial operation we opted for the largest size available, which allows us to fit various sieves depending on the flour we are making. The stones are 70cm across, enabling us to mill about 20kg per hour. It's a conscious decision for us to make really slow milled flour, as it doesn't heat up during milling, even though it's subject to lots of friction and force. So it's a really nice, cool flour. It's slow flour, also retaining more of its nutrients.

Q. What variety of wheat do you grow?
A. We are milling a German variety of wheat at the moment. We believe that because it's stone ground, and milled really slowly that it tastes a bit nuttier and earthier. The judges of the Great Taste Awards mentioned this themselves when they judged it. Both of our flours got Great Taste Awards in recent years. We farm using conservation techniques as much as possible. So we try not to plow and we limit use of fossil fuels, fertilisers and pesticides. This means we're always growing a crop even if it's only a cover crop that we don't harvest for the benefit of the soil. We like to think, even though it's anecdotal, that our crops might be more nutritious as a result of being grown in more healthy soil.

Q. With the popularity of your bread increasing, do you plan to increase your own flour production?
A. Yes. We've got the capacity to make more but it's a case of finding the right bakers. It can be quite a tricky flour to work with so they have to really want to use it. It's really quite different from what they're buying from a flour merchant. We're milling Edgar at the moment, but next summer, we might change to a different variety, which will change our end wholemeal flour.

Q. Why are you changing the variety?
A. We grow a number of different varieties. During the growing season the weather is very unpredictable, as are threats from pests and diseases. One variety might do better than another. After harvest we have them all tested and at that point we decide. We can say, "Right, that one's got the highest protein, that would be the strongest flour, so we'll use that."

Q. Is the majority of flour you mill yourself going to bakers?
A. Yes. Most of the time we sell it by the sack, supplying a few bakers in Kent. For example, Blooms in Folkestone, Daily Bread in Rusthall, Teston Bakery who are in Wateringbury, and we've just started supplying Claire's Bread, in Headcorn.

Q. Is it available for retail sale as well, in any farm shops or delis?
A. Yes. It's available in a couple of farm shops in Staplehurst, which are local to us. And also Austen's in Rochester. Apart from that, we sell at Penshurst Farmers Market and events such as Tractorfest in Biddenden, The Weald of Kent Plowing Match and Munchies on the Meadow in Cobham this year.

Q. Do you make your own bread with your flour?
A. I usually make bread about once a week, but I have to admit I use a nice bread maker, which does a really good job.

Anna's Family Kitchen

Instagram: annasfamilykitchen

Anna left a successful media career to pursue her dream of working with food. Being a passionate cook, but also a busy wife and mum of three, time was never on her side. Realising there must be thousands of people in the same position she set out to not only create delicious, wholesome and nutritious recipes for other "Waitrose Mums" (as she likes to put it) but to also make their life that little bit easier.

With an abundance of one pots and tray bakes (less washing up) she has definitely succeeded and even managed through subterfuge, to sneak in some veg the kids would otherwise not eat.

It was my vision in writing this book, that its readers would be encouraged to cook, and not only for special occasions. It was important that everyday, accessible dishes that are easy to prepare should also be included. I could think of no one better than Anna to create these for you..

Chicken, chickpea and spinach curry

The chickpeas and lentils mean this dish is packed with protein even without the meat. People have described it as a curry for people who don't like curry as it is not super hot and spicy but it is packed with flavour and is really healthy.

INGREDIENTS for 4-6

2 onions chopped	4 garlic cloves crushed
10cm fresh ginger chopped	1 red chilli deseeded & chopped
Coriander stalks chopped	1 tbsp ground cumin
1 tbsp ground coriander	2 tsp turmeric
400g can of chopped tomatoes	1/2-1 tsp dried chilli flakes
1 tbsp Garam Masala	Juice of 1/2 lemon
1kg chicken thighs	100g dried lentils
400g chickpeas	300g stock
200g spinach	1/2 tsp salt & plenty of black pepper

1. Colour the onion in a lug of oil for five mins before adding the ginger, garlic chilli coriander stalks and all the dried spices except the Garam Masala which goes in at the end.

2. Stir for five mins – it should smell amazing – then add your chicken pieces. Stir coating the chicken in the spice mix.

3. Add the stock lentils chickpeas and chopped tomatoes. Season stir then either simmer on top for 1-2 hours or put the pan with a lid on in a low oven (130 degrees) or slow cooker for 3-4 hours. The thigh meat falls apart.

4. Stir in the Garam Masala squeeze in the lemon and stir in the spinach and serve.

Mushroom Pappardelle

This is one of my favourite pasta dishes. Many years ago when I was working in media in London, long before having children (life before kids - a distant memory!) I used to order this in my favourite Italian restaurant. I played around with making it at home trying to recreate it. A lot of my recipes are inspired by dishes I've eaten out. The only change I've made over the years is to use Greek yogurt instead of cream. It costs less than £2 per head and is packed with flavour. I love Pappardelle as it holds the sauce but you could use any pasta. The dried porcini are a must - the stock they produce adds so much flavour. Try to source the widest variety of mushrooms as the different combos offer great texture, interest and flavour.

INGREDIENTS for 4

400g fresh or dried pappardelle pasta
400g mixed fresh mushrooms 2 small onions chopped
3 garlic cloves crushed   50g dried porcini mushrooms
Juice of a lemon   4 tbsp grated Pecorino or Parmesan
Greek basil or fresh thyme 4 tbsp Tims Dairy Greek Yogurt

1. Add the porcini to a bowl and cover with 100ml boiling water. Leave to soak for 10 mins.

2. Sauté the onion and garlic in a pan with a lug of oil for 10 mins.

3. Remove the soaked porcini using a fork onto a board and roughly chop. Add to the onion and garlic in the pan.

4. Add the porcini stock (try to avoid the bottom tbsp stock as it can be gritty) a generous amount of seasoning and reduce.

5. Cook the pasta according to packet instructions.

6. Add the fresh mixed mushrooms, large ones torn, to the pan and toss for 2-3 mins. Don't overlook them. They should still be firm. Add the yogurt and stir.

7. Splash a ladleful of pasta water into the mushroom pan, drain the pasta and add the pasta to to the mushroom mixture.

8. Add the pecorino and squeeze over the lemon juice.

9. Add the fresh herbs and more grated cheese if required.

Crispy Kale and Squash Salad

This warm salad is healthy but hearty thanks to the squash. I used avocado oil on this salad but you can use olive oil or rapeseed oil. I wanted to play with avocado oil having tried it at Borough Market recently and reading about it's benefits. It apparently reduces cholesterol, is high in antioxidants and improves heart health. It also tastes great! This salad also works well cold so make extra for a packed lunch the next day. You could add sliced chicken chicken. Why not grow kale and squash in your garden as they are both easy to do.

INGREDIENTS for 4

200g kale, washed and woody stalks removed
1 whole squash peeled and cubed
Maldon salt
4 tbsp avocado oil (or olive oil)
1 tsp crushed coriander seeds
1 chopped red chilli
150g pomegranate seeds
50g flaked almonds

1. Place the kale in a colander to dry.

2. Toss the squash cubes with the coriander seeds, red chilli and 2 tbsp avocado oil. Roast for 30 mins.

3. Spread your kale out on a baking tray and sprinkle with a 1 tsp Maldon salt and 2 tbsp avocado oil. Put in the oven at 170 degrees for 15-20 mins turning every 5 mins.
   When it's crisp it's ready!

Barbecued Pork with Orange, Green Beans and Pistachios

This recipe uses pork tenderloins which are lean, cheap and quick to cook. They are particularly good cooked on the barbecue or on a griddle. Many of my recipes evolve from dishes I have experienced in restaurants and on holiday. I had this combination of pork and orange this summer in Africa.

INGREDIENTS for 4

2 Kent pork tenderloins

60g pistachio nuts

200g green beans topped and tailed

2 oranges peeled and cut into segments

For the marinade:-

2 tbsp Garden of England Apple Cider Vinegar

Juice and zest of one orange

2 tbsp Worcestershire sauce

2 garlic cloves crushed

1 tbsp olive oil

2 tbsp honey

1 tbsp tomato purée

1 tsp English Mustard

1. Combine all the marinade ingredients together and spoon it over your pork tenderloins. Leave to marinade for 30 mins. They could be left all day or overnight.

2. Lift the pork out of the marinade and put in a hot pan, griddle or on a barbecue. Sear all over then spoon over half of the remaining marinade.

3. Either put in an oven at 180 degrees or move the fillets to a low barbecue spot for 15 mins. Keep turning the fillets if you are cooking them on the barbecue. Remove to a warm plate and rest under foil.

4. Pour the rest of the marinade into a saucepan and simmer for 5 mins.

5. Cook the beans for 3 mins. Drain.

6. Slice the pork tenderloin and combine with the orange segments, green beans and orange sauce. Finish with the pistachio nuts.

Pick up prawns from Sankeys Fishmongers

Prawns and Chorizo

Prawns and Chorizo work so well together. It's a great alternative to a Paella and ready in just 30 mins. I'm always determined to make the most of the broad bean season but you could replace the broad beans with peas or spinach.

INGREDIENTS:

300g raw supreme king prawns from Sankeys Fishmongers
600g Arborio rice
2 garlic cloves crushed
200ml white wine
juice of one lemon
2 handfuls Kent broad beans - try and grow your own! They're really simple. Just pinch out the tops to avoid blackfly!

2 onions chopped
300g chopped cooking chorizo
1.2 litres fish or chicken stock

1. Pod the broad beans or buy frozen ones.

2. Colour the onion for 5 mins before adding the garlic and chorizo. Stir for minute before adding the risotto rice.

3. Stir for a minute so that the rice is coated in the oil from the chorizo and add the white wine.

4. Let it bubble for a minute before adding the stock, one ladle at a time, stirring continually.

5. Once all the stock has been used, the process will take about 25 mins, add the prawns and broad beans. Squeeze in the juice of the lemon and put a lid on the risotto for 4-5 mins until the prawns have turned pink.

6. Check for seasoning and finish with fresh mint or basil.

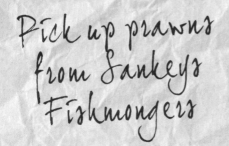

Roast Rack of Pork with Apricot and Pistachio Stuffing

If you love your crackling, you'll love roast rack of pork. The cut is basically the loin (so plenty of meat) with the bones still attached. Use two smaller racks if you're cooking for more than 4.

INGREDIENTS for 4:

1.2kg Kent pork rack on the bone
100g apricots
40g pistachio nuts
1 1/2 slices of white bread
300ml chicken stock
3 apples, peeled and cut into large chunks
100ml apple juice (we suggest Biddenden)
1/2 small onion
1 tbsp chopped parsley
1 egg whisked
1 tbsp plain flour

1. Sauté the onion in a glug of oil for 5 mins and cool.

2. In a processor whizz the bread then add the onion, the apricots, pistachios, the parsley, some salt and pepper and half the egg. Whizz adding more egg if necessary so that the mixture is firm and sticking.

3. Use a sharp knife to score the rind of the pork rack diagonally, at 2cm intervals.

4. Make a lengthways cut in the top the pork rack, close to the bones but don't cut all the way through. See the picture of the pre cooked rack.

5. Spoon the apricot mixture into flap and either tie with kitchen string (ideal!) or use skewers snapped in half like I had to as I couldn't locate my kitchen string!

6. Drizzle the pork with some oil and rub 1/2 tsp Maldon salt into the rind. Roast for 35 mins or until rind crackles at 220 degrees.

7. Reduce temperature to 200degrees. Place the apples around the pork and pour in some apple juice and drizzle over the honey. Roast for 50 mins.

8. Remove the pork from the tray and rest it for 10 mins. Spoon your apples out into a small bowl and set aside. Add a tbsp flour to your roasting tin and stir to form a paste. Add your chicken stock and hey presto you have your gravy.

Pork Tenderloin with Apples, Cider and Sage

A 30 minute one pot midweek meal using just a few simple ingredients. Any combination of apples, pork, cider and sage work brilliantly together. This dish features them all! Pork Tenderloins are very lean so make sure you don't overcook them. Serve with mash.

INGREDIENTS for 4:

2-3 Kent pork tenderloins (approx 1kg in total)
3 apples peeled, cored and cut in quarters
1 tbsp plain flour   4 large shallots halved
4 cloves garlic   500ml Biddenden cider
2 tbsp Belazu balsamic vinegar 30g pack sage leaves
1 Tbsp butter

1. Slice the tenderloins into 2cm thick pieces and toss them in the flour and some seasoning. Dust off the excess flour.

2. Warm a lug of oil in a pan and add the sage leaves to the pan in a single layer for 30 seconds to crisp. Lift them out and set aside. The sage gives the oil loads of flavour.

3. Add your shallots to the pan and colour for a few mins. Set aside.

4. Add a knob of butter and the apple pieces to the same hot pan. Colour the apples for minute before adding the balsamic vinegar.

5. Bubble for 2 mins spooning the juices over the apples to caramelise them before lifting out the apple pieces and setting them aside with the shallots.

6. Now add pork slices to the same pan. Colour them for a minute on each side. Remove and set aside with the shallots and apples.

7. Add the cider to the pan, scraping any sticky bits off the bottom of the pan and let it bubble and reduce for 8 mins so that the alcohol burns off.

8. Return the pork, apple and shallots to the pan. Simmer for 5 mins and serve with the crisp sage leaves on top.

Milk
~~Butter~~
Biddenden Cider
Garlic
Courgettes

Stuffed Courgettes

Courgettes are incredibly easy to grow and are abundant so really worth planting some seeds in the garden. What courgettes do brilliantly is take on the flavours of the other ingredients cooked with them.

INGREDIENTS for 4:

4 round local courgettes or small squash or pumpkins
(ours were home grown!)
2 red onions finely chopped
2 tsp Ras El Hanout
100g sun-dried tomatoes chopped
100g spinach
50g feta

4 garlic cloves crushed
100g quinoa
300ml vegetable stock
80g toasted pinenuts
Fresh coriander

1. Lop the tops off of the courgettes making sure you keep them for lids.

2. Scoop out the seeds and discard them. If using squash or pumpkin you could dry roast the seeds & include them.

3. Scoop out most of the flesh of the courgettes so that you have a 'bowl' about 1cm thick. Chop the courgette flesh & set aside.

4. Soften the onions in some olive oil for 10 mins before adding the garlic and sun-dried tomatoes.

5. Add the Ras El Hanout followed by the Quinoa and chopped courgettes flesh. Add all but 1 tbsp pinenuts.

6. Saute for a few mins before adding the stock. Season and let it bubble for a few mins then wilt in the spinach.

7. Spoon the mixture into the hollowed courgettes, stick their lids on and back in a hot oven in a baking tray lined with parchment for 1 hour.

8. Crumble over the feta, add the coriander leaves and the reserved toasted pinenuts and serve.

AB 566518
440

Call David
Monday morning

Sausage and Bean One Pot

This simple, healthy and comforting one pot is ready in 30 mins and comes in at less than £3 a head. Omit the sausages or replace with veggie sausages for a meat free version.

INGREDIENTS for 4:

12 Kent sausages from your butcher
2 peppers sliced
2 red onions sliced
2 tsp smoked paprika
2 cans mixed beans or beans of your choice
300g cherry tomatoes or 400g canned chopped
2 tbsp balsamic vinegar (or 100ml red wine)
200ml chicken stock
Greens - I used seasonal swiss Chard but kale, spinach or broccoli would work

1. In a hot casserole add a tbsp oil and the sausages. Colour for about 5 mins.

2. Add the onions and colour for a minute before adding the pepper, garlic and smoked paprika.

3. Add the balsamic if using or wine and simmer for a minute before adding the beans, stock and tomatoes.

4. Add some salt and pepper and simmer for 20 mins.

5. Stir in your greens to wilt. If using broccoli add 10 mins before the end of cooking time.

15 Minute Caramelised Pear and Blue Cheese Tart with Pecan Nuts

This is a ridiculously quick and easy yet professional looking tart. An effort-free lunch or dinner. The pears cooked this way are addictive - no sugar required but they're so sweet. They're great thrown into a salad.

INGREDIENTS for 4

4 firm Kent pears
180g Kent blue cheese or Dolcelatte
320g ready rolled puff pastry
2 tbsp balsamic vinegar
Tbsp butter
Handful pecan nuts
Thyme leaves
Rocket leaves

1. Core but don't peel the pears. Cut each into 4

2. Melt the butter in a pan and through in the pears. Colour on each side and add the balsamic vinegar. Caramelise the pears for 4-5 mins. The vinegar will bubble away. Set aside.

3. Lay out the pastry on a baking tray. Score a 2cm border around the edge.

4. Arrange the pears on the pastry. Sprinkle with fresh thyme, break over the Dolcelatte and sprinkle over the pecans.

5. Bake for 15 mins until the pastry is golden and the cheese is melted.

Ask any chef or home cook which single piece of equipment they couldn't do without in the kitchen and most, if not all, will nominate their trusty chef's knife. Simply put, you can't cook properly without a knife of some kind and since it does more jobs more effectively than any other tool, getting the best one you can afford is hugely beneficial. Somewhat annoyingly, what defines 'the best' is an apparently contentious topic.

As a very general rule of thumb (yet still one where you'll find strongly held opposing opinions) the more you spend on your knife, the better it is. This applies almost indefinitely in terms of aesthetics but reaches a peak around £500 or £600 in terms of utility. Other than that, it's down to personal choice. Get it right however, and you can turn drudgery into joy and save yourself a lot of time and effort through the many years you spend together.

What makes a good chef's knife?
In short materials, comfort and geometry. Sharp is good. It allows for more precision and also ensures the knife goes where you want it to. A blunt knife skidding off carrots and onion skins is exponentially more dangerous than a sharp one cutting correctly.

There are several factors to consider in choosing a good knife. It's perfectly possible to give an awful bit of steel a very sharp edge; it's keeping it that way that poses the challenge! You can help yourself enormously by learning the difference between sharpening and honing, as well as investing in a good chopping board. Most importantly find a knife with a Rockwell 'C' hardness of between 58 and 62. Much below this range the blade is too soft and will deform quickly and be reluctant to hold an edge. While too far above it and we enter the world of brittleness and blades that require the strength and tenacity of Hercules to sharpen.

You are bound to come across the phrase 'carbon steel' as a euphemism for the type of steel that rusts. All steel contains carbon (and iron), otherwise it wouldn't be steel. Stainless steel also contains varying amounts of chrome that forms a bond with oxygen and creates a corrosion-resistant surface. The amount of carbon in the steel will influence its hardness and brittleness, so one should look for a pretty solid amount. If your preferred knife manufacturer has their product description approved by their engineers, then look for a 'High Carbon' blade, as this will contain between 0.6 and 1% carbon and is perfect for a chef's knife. If the only description is provided by the marketing department, then either take your chances or look elsewhere. In the same way if you find that your chosen manufacturer uses lots of random letters jammed together to describe their steel like this: (XMov58Cr291c), then avoid.

Old myth about knives still abound. It was said that non-stainless steel is better at gaining and retaining an edge than stainless steel. Possibly 20 years ago this was true occasionally, however, this idea doesn't stand up. The best steels of both types are almost incomparable in terms of blade suitability, it's just a question of whether you want a knife that rusts or not.

Comfort and balance are hugely important aspects of a knife to consider. Held properly, a good knife will feel like you can use it for hours at a time, with neither the handle nor blade feeling heavier than the other. You may struggle to achieve this balance with cleavers and parers, for example, but a good chef's knife should balance easily on your forefinger when positioned underneath the top of the handle.

Overall weight should also be considered. A light yet robust knife is generally preferable to a heavy one. A lighter knife is less tiring and handles more easily, whereas a heavy knife is clumsy and often sees its weight trying to compensate for a poor edge. On the flip-side, a plasticky and insubstantial £10 effort will also be of not much use.

Given that making a heavy knife is a lot easier than a light one, the marketing departments are once again out in force covering for the sins of their designers. Ultimately the right feel of a knife is simply down to personal choice. If you're spending more than £100 on a chef's knife make sure you have the opportunity to hold it, experience it and, ideally, test it on a carrot.

So now we have whittled down to a knife that's sharp, and which stays that way, and which feels good to hold as well. The last and most subtle factor to consider is the geometry of the blade. Here we're talking about the cross-section of the blade, as if it were broken in half.

Almost all knives have a 'flat grind' where the sides of the blade run in a flat line from the edge of the spine to the tip. This is perfectly acceptable and is the norm simply because they are easier to manufacture. A flat blade needs to have a thin spine if it is to have a light and nimble blade but this can cause issues with rigidity if the knife is not made well. Conversely a thick spine will reward you with surer cuts and precision but it will up the weight of the knife. Additionally over time as you sharpen the knife through the years the blade will get thicker and thicker, and consequently less pleasing to use.

Some knives will have a very slightly convex grind, which will work beautifully when the knife is brand new but will degrade rapidly as you come to sharpen and remove material. The last option is for a 'hollow grind', where the knife has a concave aspect. This allows for the knife to have a substantial spine if required, while the business end of the blade will be pleasingly thin and won't thicken as you sharpen it. Sadly, very few knives achieve this optimum, as manufacture is complex and challenging.

How to care for your knife?
The efficacy of a knife is not only dependent on its manufacture but also its maintenance.
Spending a little more money on a knife will hopefully mean

you spend less time keeping it sharp. However, learning how and when to hone and, less frequently, sharpen your blade will keep your knife in tip-top condition.

Using a car as an analogy, honing a knife is like putting oil and water in your engine, whereas sharpening it is taking it in for a full service. You should aim to do the former frequently, and the latter only occasionally.

Honing requires a decent honing steel and serves to re-align the very edge of a blade after it becomes pushed out of true through frequent and inconsistently angled contact with a chopping board.

A professional chef will hone several times a day. Far from the fast-paced, theatrical, slashing technique that we often see on television, honing should be done slowly and methodically. The key is to maintain the same angle, or as close as possible, as you slide the blade's edge along the rod, alternating sides as you do so. The perfect angle will be dictated by the angle of the initial bevel made by the maker of the knife ranging from a skinny 9o for the more esoteric Japanese knives up to a chunky 25o for a flea market special. Regular honing will delay the need for sharpening, two terms which are often thought to mean the same thing, but are very different. Sharpening removes metal, honing does not.

Sharpening will generally need to be done a couple of times a year, with a whetstone being the most effective method. This is a more involved process with numerous online videos and tutorials showing how it's done properly. Even your local butcher may be willing to help out in a pinch.

As well as frequently honing the blade other day-to-day care includes keeping the wooden handle dry, applying a little linseed oil occasionally and certainly not putting the knife through the dishwasher. A wooden handle feels fantastic, but needs a bit of love: don't leave it lying around in the wet and occasionally give it a little dash of danish or linseed oil. A non-stainless knife requires much more maintenance with oil and wire wool and will be damaged if left to dry out.

Knives should be stored so as not to damage the edge. Keeping a knife in a drawer with the other kitchen tools is a sure-fire way to a dull and damaged blade. Instead, choose either a knife block, a magnetic rack or even a box or sheath.

Which knife for which task?
There are specific styles of knife, which lend themselves to particular jobs.

While the sizes and styles are practically infinite most kitchen knives fall into one of five categories, each of which has many variations:

Paring Knife
An incredibly versatile tool; designed for all those fiddly tasks which require a level of dexterity not offered by the chef's knife. Peeling, coring, topping and tailing...anything where precision is the order of the day.

Chef's Knife
The all-round, workhorse of the kitchen. This will be the knife you reach for most frequently and is the knife you're most likely to have a long lasting relationship with. Look after it and it'll look after you.

Carver/Slicer
The carver isn't a million miles from the chef's knife but generally has a longer, thinner blade for neatly carving thin slices of meat or nut roasts.

Cleaver
The cleaver is a thicker, heavier knife chiefly built to cut cleanly and easily through raw meat and bone, without damaging the blade edge. The cleaver is used throughout Asian cooking as a versatile chopping and cutting knife.

Boner
The boning knife will see most of its action working with raw cuts of meat. The thin and flexible blade is designed to get close to bones; flexing as it does so to waste as little meat as possible.

savernakeknives.co.uk

DIRECTORY OF RESTAURANTS

This book would not have been possible wihout the restaurants themsleves. I would like to thank each of them for their time and of course delicious food that I ate whilst writing this book. You are all amazing!

Angelas of Margate - angelasofmargate.com
Buoy and Oyster - buoyandoyster.com
Buenos Aires Nights - ba-nights.co.uk/
Compasses Inn - thecompassescrundale.co.uk
The Corner House - cornerhouserestaurants.co.uk
Fish on the Green - fishonthegreen.com
Folkestone Wine Company - folkestonewine.com
Fordwich Arms - fordwicharms.co.uk
GB Pizza Co - http://greatbritishpizza.com
Goods Shed - thegoodsshed.co.uk
Poet at Matfield - thepoetatmatfield.co.uk
Rocksalt - rocksaltfolkestone.co.uk
The Small Holding - The Small Holding
The Swan at West Malling - theswanwestmalling.co.uk
Thackerays - thackerays-restaurant.co.uk
The 26 Restaurant - illbemother.co.uk/thetwentysix
Three Mariners - thethreemarinersoare.co.uk
Verdigris - verdigris-tonbridge.com
Victuals & Co - victualsandco.com
Wife of Bath - thewifeofbath.com
Wyatt and Jones - wyattandjones.co.uk